mudhouse
sabbath

mudhouse
sabbath

lauren f. winner

Library of Congress Cataloging-in-Publication Data
    Winner, Lauren F.
    Mudhouse Sabbath / Lauren F. Winner.
        p.   c.m.
    Includes bibliographical references.
        ISBN 1-55725-344-7
    1. Winner, Lauren F. 2. Christian converts from
Judaism—Religious life—United States. I. Title.
BV2623.W56A3 2003
248.4'6—dc22   2003015741

10 9 8 7 6 5 4

Published by Paraclete Press
Brewster, Massachusetts
www.paracletepress.com

Printed in the United States of America.

contents

To Vanessa Ochs,
who makes these conversations possible.
Chazak, chazak.

Church, incidentally, is exactly two blocks away from Congregation Beth Israel.

It is now going on seven years since I converted from Judaism to Christianity, and I am still in that blissed-out newlywed stage in which you can't believe your good fortune and you know that this person (in this case Jesus) whom you have chosen (or, in this case, who has chosen you) is the best person on the whole planet and you wouldn't take all the tea in China or a winning Lotto ticket or even a nice country estate in exchange.

Still, I miss Jewish ways. I miss the rhythms and routines that drew the sacred down into the everyday. I miss Sabbaths on which I actually rested. I have even found that I miss the drudgery of keeping kosher. I miss the work these practices effected between me and God.

———— ✺ ————

This is a book about those things I miss. It is about Sabbaths and weddings and burials and prayers, rituals Jews and

introduction

If you call my friend Molly and no one is home, you will be greeted by an answering machine that asks, in the voice of Molly's six-year-old son, that you "please tell us your story."

Here's my story, in a nutshell: I grew up at a synagogue in a small college town in Virginia. (Congregation Beth Israel in Charlottesville, to be precise.) At sixteen, I went off to college in New York City. And then, near the end of college, I converted to Christianity. A few years later I moved back to the small college town in Virginia. Now I worship at a gray stone church that boasts a lovely rose window and a breaking-down organ and the most dedicated team of Sunday-school teachers in the South. Here at Christ Episcopal Church, I understand what people mean when they toss around that phrase "my church home." Christ Episcopal

Christians both observe, but also rituals we observe quite differently. It is about paths to the God of Israel that both Jews and Christians travel. It is, to be blunt, about spiritual practices that Jews do better. It is, to be blunter, about Christian practices that would be enriched, that would be thicker and more vibrant, if we took a few lessons from Judaism. It is ultimately about places where Christians have some things to learn.

Jews do these things with more attention and wisdom not because they are more righteous nor because God likes them better, but rather because doing, because action, sits at the center of Judaism. Practice is to Judaism what belief is to Christianity. That is not to say that Judaism doesn't have dogma or doctrine. It is rather to say that for Jews, the essence of the thing is a doing, an action. Your faith might come and go, but your practice ought not waver. (Indeed, Judaism suggests that the repeating of the practice is the best way to ensure that a doubter's faith will return.) This is perhaps best explained by a *midrash* (a rabbinic commentary on a biblical text). This *midrash* explains a curious turn of phrase in the Book of Exodus: *"Na'aseh v'nishma,"* which means "we will do and we will hear" or "we will do and we will understand," a phrase drawn from Exodus 24, in which the people of Israel proclaim "All the words that God has spoken, we will do and we will hear." The word order, the rabbis have observed, doesn't seem to make any sense: How can a person obey God's commandment before they hear it? But the counterintuitive lesson, the *midrash* continues, is precisely that one acts out God's commands, one does things unto God, and eventually, through the doing, one will come to hear and understand and believe. In this *midrash*, the rabbis have offered an apology for spiritual practice, for doing.

"Spiritual practice" is a phrase that means what it says. Madeline L'Engle once likened spiritual practice to piano etudes: You do not necessarily enjoy the etudes—you want to skip right ahead to the sonatas and concertos—but if you don't work through the etudes you will arrive at the sonatas and not know what to do. So, too, with the spiritual life. It's not all about mountaintops. Mostly it's about training so that you'll know the mountaintop for what it is when you get there.

All religions have spiritual practices. Buddhists burn sage and meditate. Muslims avail themselves of their prayer rugs. Christian tradition has developed a wealth of practices, too: fasting, almsgiving, vigil-keeping, confessing, meditating. True enough, Christians in America—especially Protestants in America—have not historically practiced those practices with much discipline, but that is beginning to change. In churches and homes everywhere people are increasingly interested in *doing* Christianity, not just speaking or believing it. Here is the place where so-called Jewish-Christian relations become practical. If the church wants to grow in its attendance to, in its doing of things for the God of Israel, we might want to take a few tips from the Jewish community.

There are, of course, some key differences between how Jews and Christians understand the doing of practice (differences that are perhaps most succinctly captured with Paul's words: "Christ, and him crucified"). The Jewish practices I wish to translate into a Christian idiom are binding upon Jews. Jews are obligated to fulfill the particularities of Mosaic law. They don't light Sabbath candles simply because candles make them feel close to God, but because God commanded the lighting of candles: Closeness might be a nice by-product, but it is not the point.

Christians will understand candle-lighting a little differently. Spiritual practices don't justify us. They don't save us. Rather, they refine our Christianity; they make the inheritance Christ gives us on the Cross more fully our own. The spiritual disciplines— such as regular prayer, and fasting, and tithing, and attentiveness to our bodies—can form us as Christians throughout our lives. Are we obligated to observe these disciplines? Not generally, no. Will they get us into heaven? They will not.

Practicing the spiritual disciplines does not make us Christians. Instead, the practicing teaches us what it means to live as

Christians. (There is an etymological clue here—*discipline* is related to the word *disciple*.) The ancient disciplines form us to respond to God, over and over always, in gratitude, in obedience, and in faith. Herewith, a small book of musings on and explorations in those practices.

Na'aseh v'nishma.

shabbat one
sabbath

Recently, at a used bookstore, I came across Nan Fink's memoir *Stranger in the Midst*, the story of her conversion to Judaism. She describes the preparations she and her soon-to-be-husband made for Shabbat:

> *On Friday afternoon, at the very last minute, we'd rush home, stopping at the grocery to pick up supplies. Flying into the kitchen we'd cook ahead for the next twenty-four hours. Soup and salad, baked chicken, yams and applesauce for dinner, and vegetable cholent or lasagna for the next day's lunch. Sometimes I'd think how strange it was to be in such a frenzy to get ready for a day of rest.*

Shabbat preparations had their own rhythm, and once the table was set and the house straightened, the pace began to slow. "It's your turn first in the shower," I'd call to Michael. "Okay, but it's getting late," he'd answer, concerned about starting Shabbat at sunset.

In the bathroom I'd linger at the mirror, examining myself, stroking the little lines on my face, taking as much time as I could to settle into a mood of quietness. When I joined Michael and his son for the lighting of the candles, the whole house seemed transformed. Papers and books were neatly piled, flowers stood in a vase on the table, and the golden light of the setting sun filled the room. . . .

Shabbat is like nothing else. Time as we know it does not exist for these twenty-four hours, and the worries of the week soon fall away. A feeling of joy appears. The smallest object, a leaf or a spoon, shimmers in a soft light, and the heart opens. Shabbat is a meditation of unbelievable beauty.

I was sitting with a cup of hot chai in a red velvet chair at the Mudhouse, a coffee shop in Charlottesville, when I read that passage. It was a Sunday afternoon. I had attended church in the morning, then cleaned out my car, then read *Those Can-Do Pigs* with my friend's two-year-old twins, and eventually wended my way down to the Mudhouse for chai and a half hour with a good book. It was not an ordinary workday, and I did feel somewhat more relaxed than I would on Monday morning. But it was not Shabbat. Nan Fink nailed it: Shabbat is like nothing else. And Shabbat is, without question, the piece of Judaism I miss the most.

It is also the piece I should most easily be able to keep. A yearning to, say, observe the Jewish new year, or a desire to hear the Torah chanted in Hebrew: Those things might be harder to incorporate into a Christian life. But the Sabbath! The Sabbath is a basic unit of Christian time, a day the Church, too, tries to devote to reverence of God and rest from toil. And yet here a Sunday afternoon finds me sitting in a coffee shop, spending money, scribbling in the margins of my book, very much in "time as we know it," not at all sure that I have opened my heart in any particular way.

God first commands the Sabbath to the Jewish people in Exodus, with the initial revelation of the Ten Commandments, and then again in Deuteronomy. The two iterations are similar, though not identical. In Exodus God says, *"Remember* the Sabbath day and keep it holy," whereas in Deuteronomy He enjoins us to *"observe* the Sabbath day and keep it holy." Elsewhere in the Hebrew Bible, God elaborates upon this simple instruction, noting in Exodus 35, for example, that no fire should be kindled on Shabbat, and in Isaiah 66 that on the Sabbath, the faithful should "come to worship before me."

There are, in Judaism, two types of commandments (*mitzvot*): the *mitzvot asei,* or the "Thou shalts," and the *mitzvot lo ta'aseh,* or the "Thou shalt nots." Sabbath observance comprises both. You are commanded, principally, to be joyful and restful on Shabbat, to hold great feasts, sing happy hymns, dress in your finest. Married couples even get rabbinical brownie points for having sex on the Sabbath.

And then, of course, are the *mitzvot lo ta'aseh*. The cornerstone of Jewish Sabbath observance is the prohibition of work in Exodus 20 and Deuteronomy 5: "You shall not do any work, you or your son or your daughter, your male or female servant or your cattle or your sojourner who stays with you." Over time, the rabbis teased out of the text just what the prohibition on work meant, first identifying thirty-nine categories of activities to be avoided on Shabbat, and then fleshing out the implications of those thirty-nine (if one is not to light a fire, for example, one also ought not handle matches or kindling).

It's easy to look at the Jewish Sabbath as a long list of thou shalt nots: Don't turn on lights; don't drive; don't cook; don't carry a pair of scissors anywhere at all (for if you carry them you might be tempted to use them, and cutting is also forbidden on Shabbat); it's okay to carry a stone or a sweater or a scarf, but only inside your own house, not out onto the street and then into the house of another; don't plan for the week ahead; don't write a sonnet or a sestina or a haiku; don't even copy down a recipe; and while you are allowed to sing, you shouldn't play a musical instrument, and of course you mustn't turn on a radio or a record player. What all this boils down to (and boiling is another thing you cannot do on Shabbat) is *do not create.* Do not create a casserole or a Valentine card or a symphony or a pot of coffee. Do not create anything at all, for one of the things the Sabbath reprises is God's rest after He finished creating.

One of the finest explanations I know of the Orthodox Sabbath comes from Lis Harris's *Holy Days,* a journalistic ethnography of a Hasidic family in Crown Heights, New York. Harris, a secular Jew, has come to Crown Heights to spend Shabbat with the Konigsbergs. She is perplexed, and a little annoyed, by all the restrictions. Over dinner, she asks her hosts why God cares whether or not she microwaves a frozen dinner on Friday night. "What happens when we stop working and controlling nature?" Moishe

Konigsberg responds. "When we don't operate machines, or pick flowers, or pluck fish from the sea? . . . When we cease interfering in the world we are acknowledging that it is God's world."

———— ❦ ————

I remember, from my Jewish days, the language we used to name the Sabbath. We spoke of the day as *Shabbat haMalka,* the Sabbath Queen, and we sang hymns of praise on Friday night that welcomed the Sabbath as a bride. It is something of this reverence, and this celebration, that is missing from my Sabbaths now.

I remember the end of Shabbat, Saturday night. By the time Saturday night rolls around, part of you is eager to hop in your car and race to a movie, go out dancing, sip a late-night espresso. But still, even after a full day of Shabbat rest and even Shabbat toe-tapping boredom (because, let's face it, occasionally Shabbat gets dull), even then you are sad to see Shabbat go. You mark the end of Shabbat with a ceremony called *havdalah*, which comes from the Hebrew verb meaning "to separate," in this case separating Shabbat from the week. *havdalah* involves a number of ritual objects—wine for tasting, and a braided candle for lighting, and a box of fragrant spices (cloves, often, and cinnamon), and you pass around the spice box because smelling the sweet spices comforts you a little, you who are sad that Shabbat has ended. One of the reasons you are sad is this: Judaism speaks of a *neshamah yeteirah,* an extra soul that comes to dwell in you on the Sabbath but departs once the week begins.

I remember that, for Jews, the Sabbath shapes all the rhythms of calendar and time; the entire week points toward Shabbat. The rabbis, who are always interested in the subtleties of Torah prose, puzzled over the two different versions of the Sabbath commandment. Why, in Exodus, does God tell us to *remember* the Sabbath, whereas in Deuteronomy He instructs *observance* of the Sabbath? One story the rabbis tell about the difference between remembrance and observance has to do with ordering time.

Sunday, Monday, and Tuesday are caught up in remembering the preceding Shabbat, while Wednesday through Friday are devoted to preparing for the next Shabbat.

What, really, was wrong with my Mudhouse Sabbath? After all, I did spend Sunday morning in church. And I wasn't *working* that afternoon, not exactly.

A fine few hours, except that my Sunday was more an afternoon off than a Sabbath. It was an add-on to a busy week, not the fundamental unit around which I organized my life. The Hebrew word for *holy* means, literally, "set apart." In failing to live a Sabbath truly distinct from weekly time, I had violated a most basic command: to keep the Sabbath holy.

I am not suggesting that Christians embrace the strict regulations of the Orthodox Jewish Sabbath. Indeed, the New Testament unambiguously inaugurates a new understanding of Shabbat. In his epistles, Paul makes clear that the Sabbath, like other external signs of piety, is insufficient for salvation. As he writes in his letter to the Colossians, "Therefore do not let anyone judge you . . . with regard to a religious festival, a New Moon celebration or a Sabbath day. These are a shadow of the things that were to come; the reality, however, is found in Christ." And Jesus, when rebuked by the Pharisees for plucking grain from a field on Shabbat, criticizes those who would make a fetish of Sabbath observance, insisting that "the Sabbath was made for man, not man for the Sabbath."

But there is something, in the Jewish Sabbath that is absent from most Christian Sundays: a true cessation from the rhythms of work and world, a time wholly set apart, and, perhaps above all, a sense that the point of Shabbat, the orientation of Shabbat, is toward God.

Pick up any glossy women's magazine from the last few years and you'll see what I mean. The Sabbath has come back into fashion, even among the most secular Americans, but the Sabbath we now embrace is a curious one. Articles abound extolling the virtues of treating yourself to a day of rest, a relaxing and leisurely visit to the spa, an extra-long bubble bath, and a glass of Chardonnay. *Take a day off,* the magazines urge their harried readers. *Rest.*

There might be something to celebrate in this revival of Sabbath, but it seems to me that there are at least two flaws in the reasoning. First is what we might call capitalism's justification for Sabbath rest: resting one day a week makes you more productive during the other six. Or, as my father has often told me, I'll get more done working eleven months a year than twelve. And while that may be true, rest for the sake of future productivity is at odds with the spirit of Shabbat.

We could call the second problem with the current Sabbath vogue the fallacy of the direct object. Whom is the contemporary Sabbath designed to honor? Whom does it benefit? Why, the bubble-bath taker herself, of course! The Bible suggests something different. In observing the Sabbath, one is both giving a gift to God and imitating Him. Exodus and Deuteronomy make this clear when they say, "Six days shall you labor and do all your work. But the seventh day is a sabbath to the Lord your God." *To the Lord your God.*

Christianity, of course, has a long tradition of Sabbath observance, so a revitalized Sabbath is more a reclaiming of the Christian birthright than the self-conscious adoption of something Jewish. Jesus observed Shabbat, even as He challenged the specifics of Mosaic Sabbath law; and since at least the year 321, when Constantine declared Sunday as Sabbath for all his empire, Christians have understood the Sabbath as a day for rest, communal worship, and celebration. New England Puritans summed up their thoughts about Sunday thus: "Good Sabbaths make good Christians."

For Christians, the Sabbath has an added dimension: It commemorates not only God's resting from Creation, but also God's Resurrection. As eighteenth-century Pietist Johann Friedrich Starck put it, "Under the New Testament, Christians also consecrate one day out of seven, Sunday, to God, that being the day on which Christ rose from the dead, and the Holy Spirit was poured out."

(Starck encouraged readers even to begin their Sabbath practices on Saturday evening, urging the Christian to "disentangle his mind from worldly cares and troubles . . . Prepare himself for the coming Sunday with prayer, . . .[and] Retire to rest betimes," so as to be punctual and sprightly at church the next morning.)

As for me, I am starting small. I have joined a Bible study that meets Sundays at five, a bookend to my day that helps me live into Shabbat—there's not enough time between church and Bible study to pull out my laptop and start working, so instead I try to have a leisurely lunch with friends from church. I have forsworn Sunday shopping (a bigger sacrifice than you may realize), and I sometimes join my friend Ginger on her afternoon visits to church shut-ins. Sometimes before Bible study, you will find me with the twins and the can-do pigs, and sometimes still you will find me at the Mudhouse. Not much, when compared to the dramatic cessations of the Orthodox Shabbat; but still, the first arcs of a return to Sabbath.

kashrut two
fitting food

Eating attentively is hard for me. I'm single, I'm busy, and I just don't give very much thought to what I eat. My most beloved cooking implement is the microwave. I hate going to the grocery store. I like picking up Thai food. Once in a while, I do a real doozy in the kitchen—risotto with portobello mushrooms, some sophisticated salad, chocolate mousse. But these bursts of culinary bravado are occasional and almost always designed to impress a guest.

As a practicing Jew, I kept kosher—which is to say I observed *kashrut*, the Jewish dietary laws. Keeping kosher cultivates a profound attentiveness to food. Because I kept kosher (the word comes from the Hebrew for "fit" or "appropriate"), I thought about the food I ate. I thought about what I was going to eat, and where I was going to procure it, and how I was going to prepare it. Eating was never obvious. Food required intention.

Only after I stopped keeping kosher did I fully appreciate that *kashrut* had shaped more than my grocery lists. It also shaped my spiritual life. Keeping kosher transforms eating from a mere nutritional necessity into an act of faithfulness. If you keep kosher, the protagonist of your meal is not you; it is God.

The laws of kashrut are found in Leviticus and Deuteronomy. As with the Sabbath laws, the rabbis embroider and elaborate the dietary code in the Talmud.

There are two basic rules:

Some foods are simply forbidden: fish without both fins and scales, creepy-crawly insects, mammals that don't chew their cud and mammals that don't have cloven hooves. This means no shellfish, no porkchops, no prosciutto, no chocolate-covered ants, no lobster bisque. No bacon with your morning omelet. No Virginia ham. (All fruits and vegetables, by the way, are kosher. Eat as many chick peas, pomegranates, Bing cherries, and green beans as you want.)

Dairy products and meat products may not be eaten at the same time. The strict separation of meat and dairy is based upon Deuteronomy 14:21: "Thou shalt not seethe a kid in his mother's milk." The rabbis interpreted that verse broadly. Not only should a baby goat not be steeped, stewed, or sautéed in its mother's milk, no meat should be cooked with any dairy product. Indeed, meat and milk may not be eaten at the same meal. Nor can a pot used to cook dairy ever be used for anything *fleishig* (that's the Yiddish word for "meat," a cognate of our word "fleshy"). So forget about cheeseburgers. Forget, also, about your plan to make cream of mushroom soup in your blue stockpot tonight: Three years ago you simmered Bolognese sauce in that pot, and now it is a meat pot forever.

In addition to those two basic principles are a host of narrower rules. Never eat blood.

Eat only animals that have been slaughtered according to Jewish law (the law requires the most painless slaughter possible, a quick and neat slash to the jugular vein). Don't eat an animal that has died of old age.

Curious rules indeed. But they are far from arbitrary. A cosmology and an ethics underpin each injunction; to keep kosher is to infuse the simple act of feeding oneself with meaning and consequence. The codes of *shechitah* for example—the rules that govern the ritual slaughter of animals for food— insist on compassion. Yes, we human beings have to kill other living creatures in order to eat, but let's make that killing as painless and humane as possible. Even the injunction about the kid and its mother's milk is symbolic. Rabbi Abraham Joshua Heschel observed that boiling a baby in the milk of its mother mocks the reproductive order and life itself. Rabbi Arthur Waskow has suggested that to separate meat products from milk products is to constantly recall a distinction between death (meat) and life (milk).

But one shouldn't romanticize *kashrut*. It must be admitted that *kashrut* can, at times, be a royal pain in the neck. Keeping kosher requires at least two sets of dishes, one for meat and one for dairy. You have to buy your brisket . and steaks and ground round at a kosher butcher. At the grocery, you'll scrutinize packaged goods, trying to determine which are certifiably kosher (Pepperidge Farm, Ben and Jerry's, and Coca-Cola all have rabbinic sanction, and most of their products are kosher; Kraft cheddar cheese and Quaker's S'mores granola bars are not). And then there's the problem of dining with your non-Jewish friends. In their homes, or at non-kosher restaurants, you're stuck drinking water and possibly munching on raw veggies. Keeping kosher is also expensive—meat slaughtered by kosher butchers is pricey, and then there are all those extra plates. Most of all, *kashrut* requires almost constant vigilance and thought. This chicken casserole calls for cream—how can I avoid the forbidden mingling of meat and milk? (For each cup of cream, substitute a cup of chicken stock mixed with one egg yolk and a dash of cornstarch.) The *Eating Southern and Kosher* cookbook suggests that you make gumbo with tofu instead of shrimp.

—⌘—

For Christians, this may seem quaint and intriguing but ultimately irrelevant. Throughout Christian history, interpreters have agreed that the moral precepts of the Old Testament—in particular, the Ten Commandments—are binding upon Christians, but the civil and ceremonial codes, from the dietary laws to the holiday injunctions, are not. And the New Testament rather dramatically makes clear that Christians are free to eat as many clams and oysters as they like: In the Book of Acts, a hungry Peter has a vision of a sheet of food descending from heaven. The sheet is filled with food that is both kosher and unkosher, clean and unclean—potatoes and chicken and spinach, but also pork chops and lobsters and prawns. A voice instructs Peter to "kill and eat," but Peter protests, insisting that he will never eat unclean, unkosher, food. The voice from heaven then says,

"What God has made clean, you must not call profane." This story is symbolic, to be sure. The voice is talking not just about food, but also about people; the instructions are not simply to eat, but also to invite both Jews and Gentiles into the Kingdom of God. Still, the story has epicurean consequences, too. Peter, a Jew who has come to follow Christ, is free to eat any and all of those once forbidden foods.

While Christians are not bound by the particularities of deuteronomic dietary law, we may still want to pay attention to the basic principle that underlies *kashrut*: God cares about our dietary choices. This should come as no surprise; you only have to read the first two chapters of Genesis to see God's concern for food. Humanity's first sin was disobedience manifested in a choice about eating. Adam and Eve were allowed to eat anything they wanted, except the one fruit they chose. And the New Testament makes clear that God cares about the most basic, quotidian aspects of our lives. (Our God, after all, is the God who provides for the sparrows and numbers the hairs on our heads.) This God who is interested in how we speak, how we handle our money, how we carry our bodies—He is also interested in how we live with food.

At its most basic level, keeping kosher requires you to be present to your food. Of course, so does the Atkins diet. The difference between Atkins and *kashrut* is God. We try out the Atkins diet because our physician cares about what we eat. We limit ourselves to kosher food—to return to the etymology, appropriate or fitting food prepared appropriately—because God cares about what we eat.

———∞———

So, down to brass tacks. I am not about to stop eating shellfish again. But I am trying to bring some thought and intention to the food I eat. The impulse comes from Judaism, but for the specifics I have turned to a number of different teachers who, though not Jewish, have an intuitive appreciation for the logic of *kashrut*.

One of my food teachers is an Episcopal priest-cum-chef, Robert Farrar Capon. In 1968, Capon wrote a slender book called *The Supper of the Lamb*. It's part cookbook, part theological meditation—something like M. F. K. Fisher meets the desert fathers. (The book is, in fact, organized around a lamb recipe, and the title's biblical allusion is not accidental.)

The second chapter of *The Supper of the Lamb* begins with the slightly absurd instruction to spend "sixty minutes or so" chopping an onion. One onion, sixty minutes. The hour is to begin with the chopper looking at the onion, encountering the onion, having a "material . . . meeting" with it. After noticing its shape, its top and bottom, its blemishes, you proceed to removing its skin, moving so carefully that you do not puncture, let alone slice, the flesh of the onion itself. And on and on Capon leads us, through a veritable onion meditation. By the end of the chapter one wonders if a single hour is enough time.

What is Capon's point? Presumably not that we should all set aside sixty minutes every time we sauté a Vidalia. Rather, he is making "a case for paying attention." After an hour with your onion, you might begin to see "that the uniquenesses of creation are the result of continuous creative support, of effective regard by no mean lover." The lover of course is God. "He *likes* onions, therefore they are. The fit, the colors, the smell, the tensions, the tastes, the textures, the lines, the shapes are a response, not to some forgotten decree that there may as well be onions as turnips, but to His present delight." And so the reminders stack up on top of one another (rather, one might note, like the layers of a cake). Food is part of God's creation. A right relationship with food points us toward Him.

Another of my food teachers is Barbara Kingsolver. In an essay called "Lily's Chickens," Kingsolver explains that she eats seasonally. When tomatoes and plums are in season, she eats them. She avoids the unseasonable temptations of modern American supermarkets, which ship in greenhouse tomatoes and lemons and plums and asparagus all year round. Kingsolver only eats tomatoes in January if she canned some back in June.

Why is Kingsolver so committed to this culinary calendar? Because shipping food from greenhouses around the world is America's second-largest expenditure of oil. (The first, not surprisingly, is our daily reliance on cars.) As Kingsolver explains, "Even if you walk or bike to the store, if you come home with bananas from Ecuador, tomatoes from Holland, cheese from France, and artichokes from California, you have guzzled some serious gas." To eat seasonally (and locally) is to enact a politics of reduced consumption.

But seasonal eating has an almost sacramental effect as well. Though Kingsolver may not have had spiritual aims when she began eating seasonally, she nonetheless introduced a liturgical calendar to her life. Her year, just like the Jewish year or the church year, now has a rhythm. Tomatoes mean summer. Potatoes and beans suggest winter. Kingsolver's seasonal diet sacralizes not just food, but time.

I do not practice seasonal eating with the rigor I once brought to *kashrut*. Last night, for example, I found myself eating a slice of pizza topped with chunks of avocado. (It's November.)

But I have begun the move toward seasonal eating. I'm embarrassed to admit that the first step in seasonalizing my diet was study. When I read Kingsolver's essay, I realized that because I am so accustomed to Whole Foods and The Fresh Market with their year-round displays of bright, perfect produce, I had no idea which fruits were in season when. I had to head to the library and read up on vegetable birthdays. (No strawberries in November, of course, but apparently persimmons are abundant here in Virginia in the fall.)

Now, like some of my Jewish friends who keep kosher at home but eat more lib-erally at restaurants, I try to keep a seasonal kitchen but allow myself to indulge when I'm out on the town. For the first time since I became a Christian, I have found myself thinking about what food I put in my body, and where that food has been—in whose hands, in what countries—before it got to my plate. Like Capon's musings on the onion, this reflecting on and participation with my food leads ultimately back to Him who sustains, provides, and feeds.

Seasonal eating is not for everyone, and it is certainly not the only discipline that can infuse Christian eating with attention and devotion. Some of my friends find that fasting one day a week imbues their six days of meals with a spirit of gratitude and joy. Others try to make all their food from scratch. Every loaf of bread is baked at home, every salad comprises vegetables from the garden in the backyard.

On Sunday morning as I watch my priest lay the communion table for the gathered believers, I remember why eating attentively is worth all the effort: The table is not only a place where we can become present to God. The table is also a place where He becomes present to us.

three

avelut
mourning

Church funerals, when they tell the truth, not only remember lovingly the lives of the departed, they also preach the gospel—they proclaim that Jesus is risen, and insist that those who died in Him shall be risen too.

What churches often do less well is grieve. We lack a ritual for the long and tiring process that is sorrow and loss. A friend of mine whose husband recently died put it like this: "For about two weeks the church was really the church—really awesomely, wonderfully the church. Everyone came to the house, baked casseroles, carried Kleenex. But then the two weeks ended, and so did the consolation calls." While you the mourner are still bawling your eyes out and slamming fists into the wall, everyone else, understandably, forgets and goes back to their normal lives and you find, after all those crowds of people, that you are left alone. You are without the church, and without a church vocabulary for what happens to the living after the dead are dead.

Mourning, maybe, is never easy, but it is better done inside a communal grammar of bereavement. Christianity has a hopeful and true vocabulary for death-and-resurrection. It is Judaism that offers the grammar for in between, for the mourning after death and before Easter.

Judaism understands mourning as a discipline, one in which the mourner is not only allowed, but expected, to be engaged. Rather than asking the mourner to paper over his grief, the Jewish community supports him in mourning. (My priest, who is always urging me to pray the despairing Book of Psalms, says that Judaism mourns well in part because Jews understand lament. "Christians," he says, "do not know how to lament.")

Jewish bereavement marks the days, and then the months, and then all the years after a death. The first space, called *aninut* (literally "burial"), comprises the days after death and before burial. During these days, mourners are exempt from the other requirements of Jewish law—they are not obligated to attend prayer services or visit the sick or welcome guests, because they are devoted entirely to the one commandment of preparing the dead for a funeral, and that preparation is all-consuming. Rabbi Margaret Holub says that mourners are exempt from other commandments during *aninut* because only the living are obligated by God's law, and in those first days after a death, mourners "border on death themselves." Even the community has different obligations during the period of *aninut*: The community is not obligated to visit or comfort or feed the mourners, explains Rabbi Holub, because until the burial, "'the death is still happening,' so the work of comforting cannot yet begin."

Then the counting starts. The next demarked days are *shiva*, or "seven," the first week after burial. In that first week, mourners "sit *shiva*." The expression to sit *shiva* is enacted literally—after the funeral, you return home to sit on low chairs, as Job's friends did; "they sat down with him toward the ground for seven days and seven nights, and no one spoke a word to him." All the mirrors are draped in black, and the mourner lights a memorial candle, and she does not wash her hair or wear perfume or put on lipstick. Mourners do not have sex, or listen to music, or wear shoes. They do not leave the house the whole seven days, except on Shabbat. Their neighbors bring food. At the first meal after the funeral—called the *seudat havra'ah*, or the meal of recovery—the mourner is meant to eat an egg, whose obvious circular fertility is to begin the slow work of reminding the bereaved that she will live.

The next unit of mourning time is *shloshim*, thirty, the first month after death. Drawn, like *shiva*, from Scripture—the captive woman in Deuteronomy weeps for her parents for thirty days—*shloshim* also makes emotional sense. It is the edging back to worldly concerns and quotidian rhythms after the intense cocoon of *shiva*. During *shloshim*, the mourner may return to waiting tables or taking depositions or folding laundry or prowling the farmers' market. But she avoids large parties and celebrations and musical performances, attends no weddings except for those of the very closest relatives.

The Talmud divides this mourning month into four discrete weeks, marked by their respective Sabbaths. On the first Sabbath, mourners attend synagogue but wait outside during the celebratory songs that welcome the Sabbath bride. (As they reenter for the remainder of the service, the congregation proclaims, "May God console you among the other mourners of Zion and Jerusalem.") On the second Shabbat, mourners participate in the whole of the service, even the joyful Sabbath hymns, but they do not sit in their usual seat, "as if to indicate," in anthropologist Samuel Heilman's words, "that even on the Sabbath, with its respite from pain, they remain somehow communally unsettled." On the third Sabbath of *shloshim*, mourners return to their regular spot in the pews, but slip out of *shul* as soon as the service ends, avoiding neighborly chit-chat. Only on the fourth Sabbath of *shloshim* do mourners become, in the Talmud's phrase, "like all people," fully participating in the Shabbat of the community.

After this thirty days comes the full year of mourning, a period designated especially for those who mourn their parents. The central commandment of mourning is to say *Kaddish*, a short prayer that begins: "Magnified and sanctified may God's great name be." It is a prayer, actually, that appears at several places in the daily liturgy—once, twice, and then a special time again, the so-called mourner's *Kaddish*. It is one of the prayers that requires a quorum of ten adults—you are not allowed to say *Kaddish* alone in your house; rather, you are permitted to recite it only with the community of believers. The mourner is obligated to say this prayer twice a day, every day, for one full year of mourning. During *shiva*, the mourner must not leave his house to go to synagogue, and so the synagogue comes to him, daily services in a living room or kitchen or den. After *shiva*, he returns to the synagogue, and there, twice a day for a year, he says *Kaddish* for his parent.

Yahrtzeit—literally, in Yiddish, the time of one year—marks the anniversary of the death. Every year, on that anniversary, the mourner lights a special memorial candle, and once again stands in synagogue to say the mourner's *Kaddish*. Some people fast. Some people give a special donation in memory of their beloved. Others visit grave-sides or study a chapter of Torah in honor of their dead. Still others take the day to look over old photographs, to raise a glass of whiskey in memory of, to recite psalms for the soul of—all different pieces of commem-orating, remembering, celebrating, and mourning.

This calendar of bereavement recognizes the slow way that mourning works, the long time it takes a grave to cool, slower and longer than our zip-zoom Internet-and-fast-food society can easily accommodate. Long after your friends and acquaintances have stopped paying attention, after they have forgotten to ask how you are and pray for you and hold your hand, you are still in a place of ebbing sadness. Mourning plateaus gradually, and the diminishing of intensity is both recognized and nurtured by the different spaces the Jewish mourning rituals create—the harrowing shock of *aninut*, the pain of *shiva*, the stepping into life and world of *shloshim*. (The rabbis would be quick to point out that we do not observe the calendar of mourning because it is psychologically beneficial, but because it is commanded—and that is true, but why should it be surprising that God commanded something that therapists might now applaud?)

Whenever I have paid a *shiva* call (the idiom may recall Emily Post, but it's just the term used to describe the communal obligation to turn up at a mourner's home and murmur comforting words), what has always struck me is the sheer crush of people. People in the den, people in the kitchen, people crowding out on the terrace and pressed into the hallway. The mourner who wants to weep in his cups alone is out of luck. On those days when he desires nothing more than to crawl back under the covers and shut out everything that breathes and has three dimensions, people pack into his home. On the last day of *shiva*, friends come and escort him, holding his arm or inching along his side, out the driveway and down the street and around the block, a symbolic (but not merely symbolic) reentry into society. Then twice a day for a year, he is forbidden to pray alone and commanded to pray with people, showing up at synagogue to do right by his dead and say *Kaddish* for them, not alone in his den but there in the community of God's faithful.

Not only is the community present for one's mourning, God is present too. God is ubiquitous in Jewish bereavement because of the *Kaddish*. Countless commentators have observed that the *Kaddish* is a curious mourner's prayer, because it says nothing about mourning. It is rather a prayer about God, describing Him as magnified and sanctified and worthy to be praised. It is not a prayer of rent garments and commemoration, but rather simply four verses of praise to God. "Blessed, praised, glorified, exalted, extolled, mighty, upraised, and lauded be the

Name of the Holy One, Blessed is He, beyond any blessing or song." As one mourner noted, the *Kaddish* is really "a Gloria." Even in the pit, even in depression and loss and nonsense, still we respond to God with praise. This is not to say that the mourner should not feel what he feels— anger, disbelief, hatred. He can feel those things (and shout them out to God; God can take it). You do not have to feel praise in the intense moments of mourning, but the praise is still true, and insisting upon it over and over, twice a day every day, ensures that eventually you will come to remember the truth of those praises.

⸺⚬⚭⚬⸺

I am still both young and lucky. My parents are alive, and my sister, and all my aunts and uncles and cousins, and even one grandparent. I can still number in the single digits the funerals I've attended, and only one of them really mattered to me, the funeral of my nearest and dearest in England, just shortly after I became a Christian. Her name was Clementine (as in the fruit, or the lost-and-gone-forever Valentine song), and she was driving on those swirling roads outside of Oxford and was killed by someone who later admitted to drinking seven or eight highballs before he got into his car.

It was sudden, of course, and horrible, and Clementine's friends and family and all the people who loved her bricolaged their way into grief. We prayed the rite for the dead. We held an all-night vigil. We sent checks to Mothers Against Drunk Driving. We sang her favorite hymns, and wore the sweaters she had loaned us and not yet reclaimed. And we put our pictures of her in picture frames, and were sad.

I described all this in an e-mail to my friend Shelby in New York. "Like all mourners," I wrote, "none of us who mourn Clementine really know what to do. It is all so shocking and unexpected and ridiculous and awful." Shelby reminded me that I might not know what to do in the face of this death, but the tradition that raised me knew what to do. "You could say *Kaddish*," she wrote.

I was not blood or marriage kin to Clementine, so, according to the particulars of Jewish law, even had I still been a practicing Jew, I was not a mourner, one who would sit on a low stool or say *Kaddish*. But my e-mail interlocutor had reminded me of the rhythm of mourning. I found, in the weeks after Clementine's death, that I did not want to listen to music, that I could not, in fact, tolerate celebration of any kind. I even found it faintly annoying when a passerby whistled or hummed. Then, perhaps three months after Clementine died, some voice in my head told me that I was overdue, that I had been sitting sackcloth for far longer than the thirty days of *shloshim*. So that night I went to hear the choir performing at St. John's College. I thought of Clementine at this concert (not something lofty like "she would have loved this ethereal music," but rather that she would have trashed the bouffant hair and vinyl fingernails of the woman sitting directly to my left).

I have not said *Kaddish*.

On the anniversary of her death, I will send another check to MADD.

I have purchased a *yahrtzeit* candle and closeted it away in my linen closet, and on October 19 I will pull it out and find some matches and remember my dead.

four

hachnassat orchim
hospitality

Few situations make me as uncomfortable
as being a newcomer in a church where I
know nothing and no one. Everyone else
knows when to stand and sit and bow and
smile, and everyone else has someone to
talk to during coffee hour, and there I stand,
awkward and ill at ease, my inner introvert
yelling at me to go home and curl up with a
novel. (This can be especially torturous at
Episcopal churches, which insist upon the
theologically sound but socially hideous
ritual of "passing the peace." Right after the
Prayers of the People and right before the
announcements, the Episcopal worshipper
is required to turn to a neighbor, shake a
hand, and say, "May the peace of the Lord
be with you." If you know your fellow

worshippers, this is a nice chatting break in the middle of the service. If you do not, you feel like a loser.)

That was how it was my second Sunday in Charlottesville. I was at Christ Church, where I knew exactly two people. (One of them was my mother, and what single woman wants to get stuck at coffee hour eating donut holes with her mom?) After the service ended, I managed to silence my introvert long enough to introduce myself to a couple sitting in the pew behind me. "Hi," they said. "So pleased to meet you." I complimented the wife's shoes, the husband asked if I'd enjoyed the sermon, and then they said, "If you don't have plans for the Fourth of July, please come to our party."

This unexpected July Fourth invitation struck me as exceptional, even though I was back in the friendly South. In the coming weeks, though, I came to see that in the Charlottesville Christian community, opening one's home seems to be *de rigueur.* To wit, the experience of my friend Suzanne: Suzanne found herself with a gap between leases, and within two days she'd had three offers of spare bedrooms from fellow parishioners.

Or consider my friends the Hanovers: So often do the Hanovers have guests for dinner that when they are guestless, eight-year-old Julianne asks, "Mommy, why is no one in the guest chair tonight?"

Or this, my favorite example of Charlottesville hospitality: One evening I attended a training session for Lay Eucharistic Ministers, those non-ordained folk who hold the chalice to your lips when you come to the altar to receive Communion. There were maybe nine of us at this meeting, and only two were this side of fifty—me, and a tall blonde man with a Georgia accent and the improbable name of Griff Gatewood (makes him sound like he's an Anne Rivers Siddons character, but he's really a real, live person). At the end of the meeting, Griff Gatewood came up to me and said, "Do you have community here with people your own age?" That is exactly what he said, verbatim. And then he invited me to have homemade pizza with him and some friends that very night. (The true confession slice of this vignette is that now the tall blonde man is my boyfriend, but that boyfriendness did not happen for months and months, so I stand by my vignette as an example of hospitality, not flirtation. He is, in fact, one of the most intentionally hospitable people I know, which is one of the many reasons I am pleased the boyfriendness happened eventually.)

After a year in Charlottesville, I have grown so accustomed to the ubiquitous hospitality that I almost don't notice it anymore. But it is noteworthy, because it is part of what the church is supposed to be: a community of people practicing hospitality.

Hospitality is not, of course, unique to Charlottesville. I first learned what real hospitality looked like from the Orthodox Jewish community in New York. In my case, what it looked like was moving to Manhattan at age sixteen and being embraced by a few families who knew little about me other that that I was new, my

family was far away, and I needed somewhere to eat lunch on Shabbat. I was never
without an invitation for Sabbath or holiday
meals. The Farmer family, in particular, held
me to an open-door policy—turn up, sleep,
eat, talk, shower, hang out, anytime, no need
to phone ahead.

In Hebrew, this is *hachnassat orchim*,
literally "the bringing in of guests."
Sociologists might suggest that Jews do
hospitality so well because they have spent
so many centuries being the stranger and the
friendless. It is also true that Jewish (and so
also Christian) sacred Scripture is thick with
the practice of hospitality. More than once,
God instructs His people to welcome the
stranger because "you were strangers in the
land of Egypt." And there is story after story
of Hebrews and Gentiles alike doing just
that. Abraham gives food to three strangers
who turn out to be angels come to announce
Isaac's birth (it is this to which the Epistle to
the Hebrews refers when it instructs, "Do
not be forgetful to entertain strangers; for
thereby some have entertained angels
unawares.") In the Book of Exodus, Jethro

was eager to welcome Moses when he sojourned through Midian. Rahab, a prostitute, was blessed for giving shelter to Joshua's spies. In 2 Kings, we read of a nameless Shunammite woman who welcomes the prophet Elisha into her home.

Later rabbinic literature surrounds the biblical stories and models with codes and instructions. Rabbi Yochanan insisted that practicing hospitality was even more important than praying. Some rabbis turn hospitality into architecture, urging faithful Jews to build houses with doors on all four sides so that travelers and guests might find a welcome door from any direction. Many Jewish communities adopted the idea of serving all their dinner courses at once; this way finicky guests would not have to suffer through an appetizer or bowl of soup they did not like.

Early Christian communities continued these practices of hospitality, attempting to feed the poor, host travelers, visit the imprisoned, invite widows and orphans to join them at mealtime—all expressions of a capacious notion of hospitality. A second-century Christian text known as the Didache instructed Jesus' followers to help visiting travelers "all you can." In a sermon on Acts, renowned fourth-century preacher John Chrysostom told heads of house not merely to delegate hospitality to their servants but to "personally welcome those [strangers and guests] who come" to your home. In the sixth century, Julianus Pomerius (sounding a little like Rabbi Yochanan) insisted that hospitality took precedence over other spiritual disciplines: He enjoined his readers to break a fast and "unbend one's self" in order to share a meal with others. The Apostle Paul placed such a high value on hospitality that he listed it—along with temperance, sobriety, and gentleness— among the characteristics required of leaders of the church.

Christians and Jews hold in common one theological basis for hospitality: Creation. Creation is the ultimate expression of God's hospitality to His creatures. In the words of one rabbi, everything God created is a "manifestation of His kindness. [The] world is one big hospitality inn." As church historian Amy Oden has put it, "God offers hospitality to all humanity . . . by establishing a home . . . for all." To invite people into our homes is to respond with gratitude to the God who made a home for us.

In the Christian doctrine of the Trinity, we find another resource for hospitality. The Trinity shows God in relationship with Himself. Our Three-in-One God has welcomed us into Himself and invited us to participate in divine life. And so the invitation that we as Christians extend to one another is not simply an invitation into our homes or to our tables; what we ask of other people is that they enter into our lives.

Some Christians have embraced hospitality with vigorous radicalism. All across the world, at places like L'Arche and the Catholic Worker houses, communities have oriented their lives toward hospitality, serving the poor and, in the most literal way, inviting strangers off the streets and into their homes.

Is, then, the Charlottesville model a bourgeois cop-out? Easy, ersatz hospitality that looks lame when held up against the hard work of all those Catholic Workers? I'm willing to entertain those arguments—and willing to cede that my friend John, who lives with and breaks bread with the working poor and unemployed in Charlottesville's housing projects, is probably earning special crowns in heaven. But the church fathers' instructions about the poor and strangers can encompass even our neighbors in the suburbs. To throw a dinner party is not to abandon the poor; it is to begin hospitality with people you know.

Not only am I a far cry from Dorothy Day, I am not even very good at luncheon hospitality. I want to be. I try to be. But I am too busy, my kitchen is too small, inviting people over takes too much time, my apartment is always too messy.

But in that list of excuses is a set of pointers about what hospitality is and is not, what it does and does not require. It does require a bit of intentionality. My lease is up next month, and I have decided to move. Among the reasons to move is space. I don't need a bigger apartment, but I need an apartment where the space is configured differently. A tour of my home will show you why. I have a huge office, and in that office sits a wonderful old picnic table, and on the picnic table sits my computer. I have a tiny kitchen, and against the kitchen wall is a writing desk that used to live in a college library. My apartment is, in other words, a great place to work, but a lousy place to eat or entertain. I almost never invite people over for dinner—their options would be to eat on the floor or eat at my desk. My new apartment, I hope, will have a smaller office and a larger kitchen, and maybe the table will fit in the room where people eat, and the writing desk in the room where people write. In other words, I have realized that I want to create a home in which friends are welcome, and my current home simply is not that. So I'm moving. (Meanwhile, if you drop by for a piece of pizza, I will crouch with you on the floor.)

Intentionality, however, is not perfection. Let's consider that very last excuse in my list, the seemingly innocent insistence that my apartment is never tidy enough for guests. Well, now. I probably shouldn't have curdling milk in the fridge if I'm inviting someone over for tea, and it might be nice if I emptied the kitchen trash can and didn't leave dirty clothes all over the bathroom floor. But to be a hostess, I'm going to have to surrender my notions of *Good Housekeeping* domestic perfection. I will have to set down my pride and invite people over even if I have not dusted. This is tough: My mother set a high standard. Her house is always immaculate, most especially if she's expecting company. But if I wait for immaculate, I will never have a guest.

God's Creation gives us a model for making and sharing homes with people, but the reality of God's Trinitarian life suggests that Christian hospitality goes further than that. We are not meant simply to invite people into our homes, but also to invite them into our lives. Having guests and visitors, if we do it right, is not an imposition, because we are not meant to rearrange our lives for our guests—we are meant to invite our guests to enter into our lives as they are. It is this forging of relationships that transforms entertaining (i.e., deadly dull cocktail parties at the country club) into hospitality (i.e., a simple pizza on my floor). As writer Karen Burton Mains puts it, "Visitors may be more than guests in our home. If they like, they may be friends."

I don't find inviting people into my life much easier than inviting them into my apartment. At its core, I think, cultivating an intimacy in which people can know and be known requires being honest—practicing that other Christian discipline of telling the truth about where we live and how we got there. Often, I'd rather dissemble. Often, just as I'd rather welcome guests into a cozy and cute apartment worthy of *Southern Living,* I'd rather show them a Lauren who is perfect and put-together and serene. Often, telling the truth feels absurd.

Not too long ago, Griff and I were at a New Year's party, attended, it seemed, by just about everyone we knew. People were sipping mulled cider and playing charades and discussing resolutions and the new leaves they would turn over, and at one point, a curvy red-headed twenty-year-old, who happened to have known Griff for a million years and who happened also to be my student, threw herself off the dance floor and into Griff's arms, for an entirely innocent, and very twenty-year-old appropriate, New Year's hug.

The next week I was chatting about some school matter with the redhead (let's call her Rita Hayworth). I was in mature, collected, professional mode—my hair was even in a chignon—and was not expecting Rita to ask, sweetly, if I had felt uncomfortable about The Hug. I wanted to sound like a grown-up. I wanted to blandly laugh and say, "No, not at all, don't be ridiculous." But some instinct told me to risk transparency with Rita H., that if I couldn't tell her the faintly lame and faintly embarrassing truth about my silly, sad emotions, how was I ever going to be able to tell the truth about something big? So I tried. I told her that actually, when she took that flying dance floor leap into Griff, I felt old and uncool and insecure, and also wondered all sorts of things about boundaries and friendship, and had wanted to kill them both. This truth-telling, to be sure, didn't change the world;

but it did push me and Rita a bit closer to real knowledge of one another.

Standing there with Rita Hayworth, I understood why Julianus Pomerius had spoken of hospitality as unbending one's self. In this unbending there was a genuine return to *hachnassat orchim*, to an inviting of guests. The irony is that the unbending requires inviting my neighbors into the very places where I am most bent.

So you see that asking people into my life is not so different from asking them into my apartment. Like my apartment, my interior life is never going to be wholly respectable, cleaned up, and gleaming. But that is where I live. In the certitude of God, I ought to be able to risk issuing the occasional invitation.

tefillah five
prayer

My first, most formative prayer lessons came at the synagogue, in the person of Ruby Lichtenstein. I was thirteen when I met Ruby, who seemed impossibly old—I think she was in her mid-fifties, but she was an old mid-fifties. She was heavy-set. She dyed her hair a color that can only be called tangerine. And she wore pastel wool suits all the time, even in summer. Perhaps an unlikely prayer teacher, but one day, shortly before my Bat Mitzvah, she took me aside and gave me a talking-to.

"Lauren," she said, "you are going to get lots of presents in the next few weeks. You are going to get earrings and *kiddush* cups and books." (She was right. Among other goodies, I received thirteen silver bracelets, two evening bags, two *challah* covers, and a copy of *Changing Bodies, Changing Lives*, a guide to puberty put out by the Boston Women's Health Collective.) "I," said Ruby, "am going to give you your most important present." The present was wrapped in a plastic grocery bag. It was a *siddur*, a prayer book. "Lauren Winner," she said, "a mark of being a Jew is praying to your God. This book is the way that Jews pray."

Jewish prayer is essentially book prayer, liturgical prayer. Jews say the same set prayers, at the same fixed hours, over and over, every day. There is, to be sure, room for spontaneous prayer (think of Tevye's off-the-cuff conversations with God in *Fiddler on the Roof),* but those spontaneous prayers are to the liturgy what grace notes are to a musical score: They decorate, but never drown out, the central theme. In the words of Jewish liturgical scholar Lawrence Hoffman, "Jews do offer freely composed prayers. . . . But overall, it is the fixed order and content of Jewish prayer that gives it its distinctiveness and that demands the personal commitment to prayer as a discipline."

Judaism is not the only religion to pray liturgically. *Salah*, the five-times-a-day Muslim prayer, is also liturgical. The American Buddhist Congress is developing a Buddhist liturgy, urging a "flexible standardization of the liturgy so that anyone attending [a] service anywhere in the country could feel at home, understand, and join in." And many Christians—in particular, Anglicans, Catholics, and the Eastern Orthodox—rely on prayer books, reciting set prayers at set hours of each day.

There are, to be sure, many styles of prayer, and I have dabbled in them all: I have prayed a rosary; I have traveled to California to walk a labyrinth; sometimes, when I am taking a walk or lying in bed or washing dishes, I chat with God as though talking to Ginger or Griff or Molly about this and that and what I wish for or fear. (On very, very rare occasions this chatting happens in the presence of other people, a three-way conversation among me and a buddy and God. One such rare occasion was dinner last week with my friend Kay. It was warm out, and Kay was smiling, wearing short-shorts and a snazzy tank top. I was a mess, fingers tapping and eyes distracted and not much sleep, worried about an e-mail exchange I'd had with my dad and wondering if I would ever know how to be a halfway decent daughter. "Well," said Kay, "we're just going to talk to the Lord about that right now." And we did—out loud, there at our wrought-iron table on the patio of the Biltmore Grill, right in front of half of Charlottesville. I am still a little bit uncomfortable with this out-loud-in-plain-view-with-other-people-right-there kind of prayer, but I am trying to learn.)

These are all good pieces of prayer, and I am glad to have them. But the skeleton that gives all these various prayings shape is liturgical prayer—the set prayers that I read every day from my prayer book. On good days, I say these prayer-book prayers at three different intervals—morning, noon, and evening. (Some days, however, are not good days, and on those days I let my morning prayers carry me all the way through to midnight.) This prayer-book praying is the way I learned to pray as a Jew. Now, as a

Christian, the prayers I say are different—
they are made in the name of Jesus; they talk
about the Holy Spirit; they often quote St.
Paul. But much of the work of the liturgy is
the same.

———∞∞———

Jews, it seems, have been saying set
prayers since biblical times. Scripture
instructs Jews to recite the *Shema*—"Hear O
Israel, the Lord your God, the Lord is
One"—upon waking and upon retiring.
Liturgical prayer became essential to Jewish
practice during the sixth century BCE when
Jews, in exile from Jerusalem, had no way to
get to the Temple to perform their traditional
sacrifices. Communities of exiled Jews met
regularly on the Sabbath and holidays, but in
lieu of Temple sacrifices, they offered God
prayers. During the next century, Jewish elders
composed the *Amidah*, or "the standing"
(because one stands while reciting it). This
prayer, made up of eighteen separate
blessings, is recited three times a day. There
is more to Jewish liturgy than the *Shema* and

Amidah; there are hymns of praise and prayers of petition and psalms. The synagogue newcomer can feel overwhelmed, but you get the hang of it quickly—it doesn't take too many weeks of reciting a prayer thrice daily before you know it as well as you know your own phone number.

It's the phone number sort of knowledge that has given liturgy such a bad rap in some quarters. "It's boring!" wails my friend Meg, who opted out of the thoroughgoingly liturgical Episcopal Church after about six months. "I tuned out. Instead of expressing my innermost feelings to God I was just reciting a bunch of old prayers by rote."

Liturgy can be dull, and its dullness can be distracting. Sometimes I set aside time specifically for prayer: I turn off the ringer on my phone and light a candle and sit in my best praying chair (the club chair with the red checked slipcover; don't ask me why, but it's generally the best); and even then I can look down at the prayer book in my hands and realize that I've been reading aloud for ten minutes, yet I have no idea what I've said. My mouth may have been mouthing psalms, but my brain was thinking grocery lists or weekend plans.

But if roteness is a danger, it is also the way liturgy works. When you don't have to think all the time about what words you are going to say next, you are free to fully enter into the act of praying; you are free to participate in the life of God.

Put differently: I have sometimes set aside my prayer book for days and weeks on end, and I find, at the end of those days and weeks on end, that I have lapsed into narcissism. Though meaning to commune with or reverence or at least acknowledge God, I wind up talking to myself about my emotions *du jour*. I worry about my mother's health, or I stress about money, or (more happily) I bop up and down with excitement about good news or sunshine or life in general, but I never get much further than that. It is returning to my prayer book that places me: places me in words that ask me to confess my sins, even when I can't think of any red-letter deeds recently committed; words that ask me to pray for presidents and homeless Charlottesvillians and everyone in between; words that praise God even on the mornings when I wonder if God exists at all. (Of course, sometimes the liturgy grandly expresses just exactly what we feel. When you have had a lousy day at work and have used every curse word you can think of to describe your boss, try an imprecatory psalm, such as Psalm 35: "May those who seek my life be disgraced and put to shame; may those who plot my ruin be turned back in dismay. . . . May their path be dark and slippery, with the angel of the LORD pursuing them.")

What I say to Meg is this: Sure, sometimes it is great when, in prayer, we can express to God just what we feel; but better still when, in the act of praying, our feelings change. Liturgy is not, in the end, open to our emotional whims. It repoints the person praying, taking him somewhere else.

———∞∞∞———

A few weeks ago, Griff and I went to Americus, Georgia. This was no run-of-the-mill trip. This was dating baptism-by-fire. During our thirty-six hours in Americus, I visited his high school, two Habitat for Humanity houses he'd helped build, and the clothing shop where he bought his first suit. I shook hands with his high school algebra teacher and his pastor (and, I'm sure, a few unidentified ex-girlfriends), and I met almost a dozen Gatewood relatives.

One of the relatives was Granddaddy Gatewood. Dr. Gatewood is, as we in the South say, in decline; and he has been declining, I gather, for the better part of a decade. He does not remember much. In the afternoon he did not remember having met me in the morning. He does not remember Griff's name, or that Anna is his granddaughter and pregnant, or the tune to "America the Beautiful," or how long it takes to get from home to church.

The Gatewoods filled an entire pew at church, and I sat near the end, between Griff and his grandfather, who sat on the end of the pew where his long legs could have some extra stretch room. Frankly, I was a little uncomfortable and annoyed. I thought it was irresponsible of Griff to stick me next to his senile grandfather with whom I had spent exactly twenty minutes. I felt that Griff and I should switch places. But I also knew better than to speak up.

And then, as so often happens when I am uncomfortable and annoyed, this seating arrangement turned out to be the best thing ever. I would later speak of the privilege of sitting next to Granddaddy Gatewood. I would say that God Himself had a hand in arranging the seating. Because sitting next to him I could see (and hear) that Dr. Gatewood, who might not even remember how to count to ten, remembered how to pray. The Lord's Prayer and the Apostles' Creed were somewhere in the foundation of his memory, beneath even his grand-children's names.

I doubt that Dr. Gatewood ever thought of what he was doing, when he said the Lord's Prayer, as "liturgy." But he was, in fact, praying a liturgy, for liturgy happens any time we repeat one prayer over and over, week in and week out. Sometimes that prayer was written by someone else (in Dr. Gatewood's case, the liturgy was composed by Jesus). Even the little child laying herself down to sleep, praying the Lord her soul to keep, is praying a liturgy. Even my friend Meg, who left the too-liturgical Episcopal Church for a praise-song-singing, spontaneous-prayer-praying charismatic church, will, I suspect, discover that she is doing liturgy: After enough time, the rhythms of the praise songs and the (seemingly) spontaneous prayers will become familiar and even routine, a liturgy of its own.

One could, I suppose, ask some questions about Dr. Gatewood's praying. Did he understand the propositions he was asserting in the Creed? Maybe not, but then on many days I don't understand them either. I don't know whether he could have cogently analyzed the Lord's Prayer or explained the Trinity to whom it was directed. What I know is this: These words of prayer are among the most basic words Dr. Gatewood knows. When he has forgotten everything else, those words are the words he will have. Those words have formed his heart, and—regardless of what he feels or remembers on any particular morning—they continue to form his heart still.

guf body

I am downtown, outside a little boutique called Pearl, a boutique I hardly ever enter because their clothes, like the biblical pearl, come at great price; but this particular day I am strolling around with Ginger and we notice the Pearl mannequin is sporting a most cute skirt. It is just past the knee, pale cotton affixed with grosgrain ribbon, sporty, summery, and oh-so-chic. "Oh, try it on," says Ginger. The skirt costs $182. "If I knew how to sew," I say to Ginger, "I could make that skirt for twenty bucks." "But you don't know how to sew," says Ginger, "so try it on."

I do. "This small does not fit," I sing to the saleslady. "Do you have a medium?"

The saleslady (I am sure she is sighing and rolling her eyes and annoyed) goes to the mannequin, which is wearing a medium.

"The medium," I say, "is a little snug." Actually, I cannot get it to zip.

This is the sort of store that does not carry a large.

"Ah, well," I say cheerfully, "think of the $182 dollars I just saved, thanks to my hips, which were designed to have babies." Then, when we are out of the store, I start to cry.

"Why are you crying?" says Ginger, who knows why I am crying.

"I'll never be thin again," I wail. "I used to be thin." I tell Ginger about the purple pedal-pushers I had just taken to Goodwill because they, too, were a tad tight. Ginger reminds me that I bought the pedal-pushers in tenth grade.

This shopping expedition was good proof that, though I believe God has something to say about human bodies, I generally tune God out and listen to *Cosmopolitan* instead. I'm pretty sure that God, if He called me to chat about my body, would say things like, "I like your body. I created your body, and if you have read the first chapter of Genesis lately, you might recall that I called Creation good." Still, when I'm staring in the dress-shop mirror, I generally wish my body— or at least a few pounds of it—would vanish.

This desire to diet is not just bad feminism. It is also bad faith, for the biblical story of the body is very different from the bodily stories *Cosmo* and *Maxim* tell. The magazines (and movies, TV shows, and advertising campaigns) speak of bodies that are both too important and not important at all. Scripture speaks of bodies that God created in His image, bodies that are both doing redemptive work and being redeemed.

Christians, it must be admitted, have not told that story very consistently. The history of Christianity and the body is one of anxiety and unease; Christianity has the words to offer a spirituality of the body, but the church hasn't always spoken those words.

Judaism, on the other hand, has much more clearly insisted that being a body is intimately bound up with being a follower of God. This understanding is expressed in one of the most basic Jewish rituals, the *bris*, the ritual circumcision of baby boys. God commanded circumcision in Genesis 17 as a sign of the covenant between Abraham and the Lord, and in circumcision, Jews mark their bodies for God. Jews carry the marks of their covenant with Him in their very flesh. The *bris* suggusts that we do religion with our souls and hearts and minds, but we also do religion with our bodies.

Judaism offers opportunities for people to inhabit and sanctify bodies and bodily practices. Jews link everyday bodily practices, like eating and drinking, to the service of God. Judaism even sees the undeniably bodily acts of urinating and defecating as an opportunity for spiritual growth. Jewish law—which generally encourages one to think about lofty, holy things at all times— forbids contemplating the sacred while in the bathroom. The *Shulchan Aruch*, the sixteenth-century codification of Jewish law, reminds readers that "while in the bathroom, it is forbidden to think of sacred matters. It is, therefore, best to concentrate on your business affairs and accounts, so that you might not be led to think of holy thoughts, or, God forbid, indulge in sinful thoughts. On the Sabbath, when it is forbidden to think of business, you should think of interesting things you have seen or heard about, or something similar." Still, the rabbis are eager to transform the bathroom experience into one that can edify and point toward the Creator. Says Rabbi Yehudah ha-Hasid, "When you are in the bathroom or bathhouse, remember how much uncleanness and filth exits from your body, and be humbled."

Judaism connects physical acts to spiritual practice without somehow suggesting that the spirit is superior to the body. Consider sex. Rabbinic sources suggest that the intention of sexual intercourse is unity with one's spouse and with God; but Judaism's recognition of the spirituality of sex does not come at the expense of sexual physicality. One rabbi made the point plainly: Before sex, he taught, you should give thanks to God for the pleasure that He created.

The same holds for eating. As Rabbi Abraham of Slonim taught, "Contrary to what one might think, it is possible sometimes to come closer to God when you are involved in material things like eating and drinking, than when you are involved with 'religious' activities like Torah and prayer. Because when the heart opens up due to . . . pleasure . . . then is the fit time to come close to holiness."

Jews connect eating to God, not just through the dietary codes of *kashrut* but also in the preparation of tables and meals. The table laden with food is meant to recall the altar of the Temple. (This has practical consequences that will be pleasing to moms everywhere: According to a Hasidic teaching, even clearing the table after a meal is a holy act, for it recalls the priests' removing sacred spoons from the Holy of Holies.) Every morsel of food is blessed before being eaten, and Jews recite a lengthy grace after meals. A consistent theme in the traditional literature on eating is that the pleasure of good food can point back toward the Creator. There is a Hasidic tale of a rabbi who visited a very poor woman. She served him dinner, and the food was scrumptious. The rabbi, having enjoyed the meal tremendously, looked at the woman and declared, "This food tastes like heaven!" Smiling, the woman said, "That's because while cooking I prayed that God would put the taste of the Garden of Eden in the meal." Physical pleasure provided a foretaste of eternity.

The point is not that we'll know God simply because we experience fine dining. Jews know God because He has revealed Himself in the covenants, not in meals. Jews can appreciate meals, sex, and the body because they already know the God who made Creation. Because one knows the Creator, one can taste Him in the breaking of bread.

It is no accident that Jewish prayers relating to the body acknowledge, above all, God as Creator. The prayer to be uttered before sex thanks God for creating pleasure; similarly, the *asher yatzar*, the blessing Jews recite after going to the bathroom, thanks God for "creating in me many orifices and many cavities. It is obvious and known before Your throne of glory that if one of them were to be ruptured or one of them blocked, it would be impossible for a man to survive and stand before You." Jews can be present to their bodies in part because they have a story, and a doctrine, of Creation.

One must acknowledge an underbelly (to use a bodily metaphor) to this sanguine picture of Jews and bodies. Jews engage their bodies not simply because Jewish theology, the Jewish teaching of Creation, suggests they ought, but also because the non-Jewish world has engaged Jewish bodies pathologically and prejudicially. Ideas about Jewish bodies have figured prominently in anti-Jewish and anti-Semitic tropes for centuries—beginning with the Christian idea, put forth most notably by Augustine, that Jews were inherently and basely corporal and bodily; their very carnality prevents them from apprehending the spiritual reality that is Jesus Christ. A more modern anti-Jewish topos insists on a particular Jewish physiognomy—the hooked nose, the full lips. In America, Jewish women's bodies have become the stuff of anti-Jewish fantasies; in a

1930 New York newspaper, to cite just one example, an anonymous columnist at once insisted that Jewish women spent more money on clothes and accessories than their Gentile counterparts, and excused Jewish women for the extravagance because "the Jewish girl must offset her . . . vulgar [figure] by making it her rule to wear the simplest clothes possible. [And] alas . . . the simplest clothes are the most expensive." If Christians have not developed the same vigorous enjoyment of the body that Judaism cultivates, that is surely in part because Christians have not been pushed, by caricature and perversion, to define, defend, and revel in their bodies.

Still, it is curious that Christians, in contrast to Jews, have such ambivalence about the body. The difference between Jewish and Christian understandings of the body is not as simple as the popular stereotype that Christians think the body is bad and Jews think the body is good. Rather, as scholar Daniel Boyarin puts it, "for rabbinic Jews, the human being was defined as a body—animated, to be sure, by a soul," whereas for early Christians "the essence of a human being is a soul housed in a body." Later Christians perpetuated an uneasiness about bodily matters, and by the modern era, Western Christians had become very much an Enlightenment people who liked to live Christianity in their minds rather than in their bodies. True enough, the church fathers labeled Gnosticism, with its insistence that spirit was separate from and superior to matter, a heresy; but, like most great heresies, Gnosticism has mutated and morphed and continued to dog Christianity. Even the most faithful Christians can sometimes catch themselves in a Gnostic mindset of wanting to deny, rather than rightly order, bodily desires for sex, food, even sleep.

This Christian discomfort with the body perplexes me. Christians, after all, share the story of Creation that seems to have provided Jews a rich resource for a robust realization of the body. And we have another story, too: the bodily Incarnation and bodily Resurrection of God. The New Testament makes clear that God cares about bodies very much indeed. He created us with bodies, He incarnated and took on a body, and He was resurrected in a body. We will be these bodies, albeit transformed, in the final Resurrection. Bodies are not mere trappings. They are the very stuff of us.

Attending Christianly to our bodies is a matter of some urgency, because there is no neutral way to be a body. If we do not take our bodily cues from the Christian story, we will take them from somewhere else—from the magazines screaming about taking off five pounds, from the all-you-can-eat buffets asking us to stuff our bodies, from the fashion designers asking us to parade them.

Yet to think of Christian practices of the body seems almost to ponder a contradiction in terms. In church, I sometimes kneel and raise my hands and bow my head. I decorate my body with cruciform jewelry. That's about it. I have not, apparently, managed a Christian attitude toward skirt size.

What I want is to pay more attention—and more explicitly theological attention—to my body and the things it does every day and the connections between the work of my body and the daily service of God. On the occasion when I linger over a meal for more than eight minutes (and it's no coincidence that those lingering evenings are also the evenings that I don't eat alone), supper, like the Communion table, can be an opportunity to meet God in the breaking of bread. Similarly, Disciples of Christ minister Stephanie Paulsell has suggested that we take our evening bath as an opportunity to ponder and pray into the baptismal covenant. I think this is a grand idea, although I haven't managed to implement it—to be honest, most days when I settle into my lavender bath foam, the last thing I'm thinking about is the morning I stood in the Clare College Chapel, renounced Satan, and accepted Christ.

Another realm to which the gospel might speak is exercise. Some Christians may cringe at the old Pauline insistence that "our bodies are the temple of the Holy Spirit"— the phrase has been so oft repeated as to seem trite, if not entirely denuded. But I must confess there are only two reasons I get up for my 7:30 exercise class: the knowledge that my friend Molly is there and will kill me

if I don't show up, and the equally sure
knowledge that Scripture enjoins me to care
for my body. Does this mean that I think
about Jesus with every jumping jack? Not at
all. What it means is that my exercising is
not merely a capitulation to a fitness-crazy
culture, but rather is an attempt at obedience.
God created this body of mine; the least I
can do is try halfheartedly to take care of it.
(Granted, I do this only once a week. God, it
seems, is not finished transforming sedentary
me into a new creature.)

Then there is the matter of suffering. It is
all well and good to urge Christians to be
present to their bodies when they are eating
a good meal or having great sex. But what
does it mean to preach presence to one who
is in bodily pain?

Lately, I've been thinking about bodies in
pain, principally because I've been watching
my mother's body deteriorate. She has
uterine cancer—an especially invasive and
aggressive kind of uterine cancer. The good
news is the chemo seems to be working. The
bad news is that when chemo works, the
oncologists keep giving it to you, injecting

you with just the right amount of poison
(they hope) to kill the tumor but not kill
you. First, naturally, her hair fell out. Then
she simultaneously lost weight and got
bloated (a sad thing to watch happen to the
body of a woman who won legs contests in
college). Then came peripheral neuropathy;
in layman's terms, she has lost the feeling in
her feet. She has begun to walk with a cane and
has traded in her stick shift for an automatic.

I want her to read this chemo and cancer
through gospel lenses—even as I am not
entirely sure what that reading would look
like. This is not to say that suffering is a
Christian good, that suffering makes us holy
and puts us closer to God (though, sometimes, making us holy may be one thing that
suffering accomplishes). I remind her that
the Incarnation culminates with Christ
suffering on the Cross. When God became
man He did not simply take on a body that
was in the bloom of health. He took on a
body destined for suffering, and His body
now, as my mother's body one day will be, is
resurrected and in heaven. The irony, I suppose, is that sometimes it may be our very

bodily suffering that forces us to inhabit the bodies our culture has helped us alternately vilify and ignore. Catholic poet and memoirist Nancy Mairs has made the point when writing about multiple sclerosis: "Slowly, slowly," she writes, "MS will teach me to live as a body."

The latest side effect of my mother's chemo is cosmetic: Her eyebrows have fallen out. (One lone brow hair remains over her right eye, and she takes this as a metaphor for tenacity.) Mom has penciled in orange crescents where her eyebrows should be, and when she asks if these new brows are too terribly obviously fake, I tell her it is nice that the bangs of her wig are so long.

I used to nag my mother about make-up. She is one of those Southern Ladies of a Certain Age who spend a good chunk of the morning preparing her face to meet the world. I've always found this ridiculous, and so once I confiscated all her lipstick. I tried to get her to read *The Beauty Myth*. To no avail.

Part of me still wishes she would take to the streets bald—some sort of political statement about women's health and women's bodies. But I am beginning to understand about the dignity and the art of the wigs and the makeup. This small, everyday attentiveness of eyebrow pencils is perhaps a picture of the very sort of bodily care our embodied God would have us cultivate whether in illness or wellness, whether our bodies are in the throes of ecstasy or the throes of pain.

seven

tzum
fasting

My priest has tried, on a few occasions, to talk to me about fasting. Was regular fasting part of my spiritual discipline? Did I fast on Good Friday? Did I fast on Ash Wednesday?

"I'm not really into fasting," I would say. "I don't know why fasting is so hard for me," I would sometimes add with an air of world-weariness. "When I practiced Judaism, of course, I fasted all the time."

Once, my priest tried to give me an out: "So do you think the reason you don't fast now, as a Christian, is because there is still an emotional tie, or a symbolic connection, or maybe just some unfinished business to do with Judaism?"

"Nope," I said, "I just don't really like to do it. To fast, that is."

Eventually, these conversations had to end, and the way they ended, finally, was my agreeing to try to fast on Fridays during Lent.

Fasting, in Judaism, is a given. On holidays such as the Day of Atonement or the Ninth of Av (which commemorates the destruction of the Temple), all observant adult Jews fast. Indeed, the Jewish calendar designates no fewer than seven days that should be set aside for fasting. These fast days fall into one of two categories, the major fast and the minor fast. On a major fast, like the Day of Atonement, you fast a full twenty-five hours, from sunset to sunset, and you abstain not only from food and drink but also from anointing yourself and from sex. Also, you do not wear leather shoes, because leather is too comfortable for a fast day. This is why you will see many Jews in synagogue on the Day of Atonement, the holiest day of the year, dressed to the nines and wearing white tennies. The minor fast is shorter, just sunup to sundown, and only prohibits food and drink. And there are exceptions, of course. If you are ill, or pregnant, or nursing, or too elderly, or too young, you do not have to fast. If the fast falls on a Sabbath, it is suspended (except for Yom Kippur, which is the Sabbath of Sabbaths, and takes precedence even over the commandment to be joyful on Shabbat).

To be honest, I was never all that good at fasting. I generally kept the fasts, but I rarely seemed to do them well. Fasting is meant to take you, temporarily, out of the realm of the physical and focus your attention heavenward; as one Jewish guide to fasting puts it, "at the heart of this practice is a desire to shift our attention away from our immediate needs and to focus on more spiritual concerns." But I usually found myself more, not less, obsessed with my belly. And, once or twice, I skipped or ignored or broke a fast. My freshman year of college, for example, I got distractingly hungry on the Fast of Esther. And so at about two o'clock I ate a salami sandwich. Actually, the story is worse than that: Not having any food in my dorm room, I found the key to the campus kosher deli where I worked (it was of course closed because of the fast day) and made my salami sandwich there.

——————— ∞∞∞ ———————

There is a long history of Christian fasts, beginning with those fasts observed by Jesus Himself. Jesus' most stunning fast came in the desert, where He fasted for forty days. At the end of the forty days, the devil came and tempted Him with power and glory and riches, and Jesus withstood the Adversary, saying "Get thee behind me, Satan." The Gospel of Luke suggests that though perhaps physically weakened from His fast, Jesus was spiritually much stronger for it, and, indeed, the fast helped give Him the moxie to renounce the devil. A curious and paradoxical-seeming, even impossible-seeming, lesson: fasting won't just make you headachy and irritable and ravenous. It will make you, somehow, stronger. Jesus seemed to assume that fasting was an essential part of the spiritual life—He said to His disciples,

"When you pray, when you fast, and when you give alms," not *if* you fast, but *when*. And the Gospel of Matthew makes this scary, flat claim: There are demons that "go not out but by prayer and fasting."

Fasting was a central discipline to the early church and on through the Middle Ages, but people fell away from fasting after the Reformation. At least in Protestant churches, fasting has been generally reduced to Lenten observance—some people abstain from food on the Fridays of Lent; others make a mini-fast for the entire period, giving up chocolate or alcohol or restaurants. The strong hold of the Lenten fast returns to Jesus in the desert, for during Lent we both recall and recapitulate His forty days there. During Lent we also repent, and as the rabbis say, fasting is at its core about repentance.

Though since the Second Vatican Council American bishops have stripped the act of obligatory status, many Catholics have retained the practice of abstaining from meat on Fridays. These Friday fasts recall, weekly, the suffering of Christ on the Cross. Eastern

Orthodox Christian communities, it seems, understand and inhabit fasting best. During Lent, for example, they completely abstain from all meat, dairy, and egg products. The Orthodox also fast on Sunday mornings, refraining even from drinking a cup of coffee until they have partaken of Holy Communion, feeding on the body and blood of Christ before they indulge in a croissant or a stack of pancakes.

In recent years some American Protestants have begun to recover this venerable Christian practice. As journalist Christine Gardner has written, "American evangelicals [are] rediscovering fasting, among the most ancient and rigorous of spiritual disciplines." Whole communities have taken up fasting for repentance, fasting for discernment, fasting for purification. Two examples will illustrate: In 1998, two million people tuned in, via the Internet, to a Campus Crusade for Christ conference on fasting and prayer, and the following year the National Association of Evangelicals promoted forty days of fasting and prayer for its 43,000 member churches.

Contemporary Christian enthusiasm for fasting has included a creative and capacious notion of what it means to fast. Increasingly, Christians think of fasts not simply as abstentions from food, but abstentions from all manner of indulgence. Catherine Marshall, the charismatic writer best known for her novel *Christy*, once fasted from offering criticism. In *A Closer Walk,* she describes her surprise at the number of times she simply had to stay silent because she had nothing non-critical to say, and then again her surprise at how little her usual contributions were missed. (Though Marshall probably wasn't thinking of it, there is a medieval Jewish precedent for her criticism fast—the *tzom shtikah*, or the fast of silence, in which Jewish mystics refrained from speaking, and, in their stillness contemplated the mysteries of the divine.)

These non-gastronomic fasts can, no doubt, be edifying and instructive, but I suspect that a criticism fast, however difficult, would be easier for me than a food fast, and I suspect that I would be pretty tempted to use the cunning and spiritual-sounding criticism/TV/shopping/etc. fast as a justification for avoiding the basic discipline of abstaining from food.

—∞∞∞—

So my priest has asked me to fast on Fridays during Lent, and that is what I have tried to do. Some Fridays are better than other Fridays. Some Fridays are okay, and other Fridays are irksome. One Friday I got a headache I couldn't shake. On another Friday I scooped out half a bowl of chocolate chip ice cream before I remembered. On still another Friday, I seemed to be praying better than I had prayed in a long, long time, but I am not sure that the fast had anything to do with the fortitude of my prayers: It might be coincidence. People who have fasted for years tell me there will come a time when I look forward to fasting—they tell me that there will come a time when I chafe under the church's insistence that one not fast during Christmas or Easter, seasons wholly given over to feasting. I am willing to believe that those times may come, but they are not here yet.

There are, of course, practical ways to make fasting less difficult. I have figured out that I always get hungry around two o'clock (the Hour of the Salami Sandwich), and if I'm willing to sweat it out till about 3:30, I'll be okay until dinner. And my beloved priest has told me that, just as Judaism makes allowances for circumstances that would make fasting too burdensome, so does Christianity. Not simply if you are sick or nursing or infirm, but also, says my priest, if you are unavoidably with people. That is to say, when your grandparents are passing through town and expect to take you to Bizou for lunch on Friday, you are to suspend your fast and go to Bizou, because going is the hospitable thing to do, and the communal practice of hospitality, judiciously understood, trumps your own private devotion.

Even in this early relearning of fasting, I can begin to see that Jesus expects us to fast not because He is arbitrary or capricious or cruel, but because fasting does good work on both our bodies and our souls. One Jewish fasting manual instructs its readers to slow down during fast days, to accept that our bodies will not move and our synapses will not click and our brains will not process quite as quickly. (In this way, "fast" sometimes seems like a misnomer.) It's a basic point, but one that bears repeating: Fasting is to be, as St. Thomas Aquinas once wrote, "a perfect quieting of all our impulses, fleshly and spiritual." Fasting is not meant to drag us down, but to still us. It is not meant to distract us from the really real, but rather to silence us so that we can hear things as they most truly are.

After that salami sandwich Fast of Esther episode, I rang up my rabbi. I asked him how important these minor fasts were. I asked him if I would ever get any better at them. I asked him what the point was. "Take Yom Kippur," I said. "Yom Kippur is the holiest day of the year. It is a day during which you should focus every iota of your attention on God. Wouldn't it be easier to do that if you had eaten a bowl of cereal at nine A.M., and so weren't thinking about your hunger pangs all day?"

Rabbi M. did not roll back thousands of years of rabbinic instruction and tell me to eat a bowl of Chex on the morning of Yom Kippur. Instead, he said the hunger was part of the point. "When you are fasting," he said, "and you feel hungry, you are to remember that you are really hungry for God."

And that has become my litany, my chant. When I sit at my desk on a Friday afternoon and wonder whether one little blue corn tortilla chip with a dab of black bean spread would really hurt, I say the words out loud: *I am hungriest for God, my truest hunger is for God.*

That litany tells me what fasting is. It is not merely a long, torturous means to a far-away end; a fast is not to be understood as a miserable experience that will eventually sanctify you. Nor is a fast like a back-room deal at the courthouse, the lawyer for the penitent trading three weeks of food in exchange for divine mercy. Rabbi M.'s words make clear that, like the liturgy, the fast accomplishes a repositioning. When I am sated, it is easy to feel independent. When I am hungry, it is possible to remember where my dependence lies.

eight

hiddur, p nai zaken aging

"Do you have a section on aging?" I asked the woman at the information desk of the bookstore. I had already searched the health, family, and self-help sections. I was looking for a book for Lucy, a seventy-two-year-old woman I sometimes visit. She had read May Sarton's *At Seventy* and asked me to bring her something else in that vein.

"Nope," said the cheerless bookseller. "No aging section, but we do have quite a few books on aging over here." She led me to a bookshelf marked "beauty." There, jumbled up amongst *Beauty Secrets for Dummies* (foreword by the Duchess of York) and *The Beauty Bible,* were, after a fashion, a bunch of books about getting old: books with titles like *Battling Your Wrinkles* and

Looking Phenomenal after Fifty. "These," I said, "seem to all be books about fighting the cosmetic effects of aging." I flipped one open to a discussion of age-spot removal: "Try lemon juice," the book instructed, as though written for a pre-teen nervous about freckles. I did not think age-spot removal was what Lucy wanted.

There is a *midrash* that speaks to this impulse to lemon-juice away your age spots. Once upon a time, the *midrash* says, adults of all ages looked the same—there were no crows' feet, no flabby upper arms, no sagging breasts or thinning hairlines.

But eighty-year-olds passing for thirty posed a problem: Whenever Abraham and his son Isaac went out together, no passersby could tell that Abraham was the elder—and since they couldn't tell he was old, they couldn't offer him the honor and reverence due to the elderly. So Abraham asked God to "crown him" with age spots and gray whiskers.

That *midrash* tells us something of how Judaism traditionally understands aging. The aged are not to be dismissed or ignored, but honored. Indeed, so central is that notion of honoring our elders that it finds its way to the middle of the Ten Commandments: "Honor thy father and thy mother." The same sentiment is reiterated and made more general in Leviticus 19:32 (NIV): "Rise in the presence of the aged, show respect for the elderly and revere your God."

Over the centuries, the rabbis have spelled out just what "respect" and "honor" require. The young are not to contradict, anything their elders say. We are to stand whenever in the presence of someone who is elderly, even if that person is not especially wise or good or learned. Thirtysomethings are not permitted to take the most comfortable chair or sofa, but are to leave it empty in case an older person should enter the room.

A contemporary Jewish poet, Danny Siegel, has offered a creative reading of the biblical injunctions about the elderly. Poetic license firmly in hand, he translates the verse in Leviticus: "You shall rise before an elder and allow the beauty, glory, and majesty of their faces to emerge." We are obligated, says Siegel, "to provide whatever is best suited to the personal needs and desires of the elderly."

That may mean something simple, like bringing your older neighbor the latest John Grisham in large print or heading to Target and buying one of those digital alarm clocks with the honkingly huge red numbers for your dad. Or providing for the elderly's needs may be more demanding. It may mean caring for them at home while they die. It may mean, as it meant for my grandmother thirty years ago, converting your empty-nest spare bedrooms into an apartment for your elderly mom. It may mean, as it meant for my sister, driving that same grandmother, now an octogenarian, to Florida the year she finally decides she probably shouldn't drive herself.

It must be acknowledged that this giving care can be burdensome. It can be draining and hard. Perhaps the most essential insight of the Jewish approach to caring for one's elderly is that this care is, indeed, an obligation. What Judaism understands is that obligations are good things. They are the very bedrock of the Jew's relationship to God, and they govern some of the most fundamental human relationships: parent to child, husband to wife (and wife to husband, of course).

Somehow, though, when it comes to caring for the old, we disdain the notion of obligation. In one book I read recently, for example, the author explains that when she grows old, she hopes her children will spend time with her only when they want to: "I don't ever want to be an obligatory visit on my loved one's calendars. . . . Whenever Robin and Edward visit Gramy Gert . . . they do so with no sense of duty. They look forward to spending time with her." I am thrilled that Robin and Edward enjoy their time with their grandmother so much, but the simple reality is that caring for our elderly, just like wiping our babies' bottoms and forgiving our spouses, is not always going to be something we look forward to.

My mother is not yet elderly, but she is sick, and her cancer has required some caretaking on my part. To be honest, I don't usually enjoy folding her laundry or flipping her mattress or running to the pharmacy for her prescriptions, and I don't always enjoy visiting with her. I do not look after Mom because it is consistently easy and delightful. I do it because I am obligated. I do it because of all the years she looked after me. This is a sort of holy looking-after. It is not always fun, but it is always sanctifying. And in this way, perhaps, caretaking is something of a synecdoche of the spiritual life: Most good and holy work (like praying and being attentive and even marching for justice or serving up chili at the soup kitchen) is sometimes tedious, but these tasks are burning away our old selves and ushering in the persons God has created us to be.

Plus, of course, caring for another person can sometimes be exceptionally straight forwardly rewarding. It can sometimes be the best thing ever. Tonight I stopped by the health-food store and decided to buy my mother an avocado. It is just a small piece of green fruit, and it might not even appeal to her chemo appetite, but it was good and simple and even joyful to bring it home to her all the same.

———————

We young folks are supposed to care for and respect our elders—that is the starting point for both Jewish and Christian teachings about the old. But both traditions also speak to those who are aging themselves. The elderly are asked to age well, and the communities that support them are asked to help them do just that. (Rabbi Zalman Schacter-Shalomi has dispensed with the gerund "aging." He speaks instead of "eldering." I'll admit a certain squeamishness with the term—it strikes me as a little twee, and every time I think of it, I have to adjust. But there is something vigorous about it too. To age is to be passive, to sit like a bottle of wine— you just sit there and time passes and age happens over you. To elder—or, in another of Reb Zalman's clever infinitives, "to sage"— is to try to shape the last years of one's life with intention.)

Aging is not just a process of physical decline. It can also be a time of the kind of stripping away that fosters spiritual depth, spiritual incline. The Hebrew word *sayvah,* gray—as in gray hair—is etymologically connected to the word for repentance, *teshuva:* The process of aging, then, is the process of setting wrong things right.

In the Middle Ages, in particular, Christians spoke of aging as, in the words of historian Shulamith Shahar, "an opportunity for spiritual elevation." John Bromyard, author of a fourteenth-century preaching guide, was not unique in holding the view that "in so far as old age reduces . . . youthful vigor, it increases the soul's devotion to God." Twenty-first-century Christians should not, perhaps, adopt the medieval view without criticism—the medieval thinker's understanding of the aging body was bound up with ambivalence about all bodies. Nor should the spiritual opportunities of aging distract the church from the sometimes difficult social and economic realities that face the elderly. Still, at the core of the medieval vision is the understanding that aging is not just about joints and wrinkles and families and hearing aids.

It is also about prayer and attention and preparation and God.

The spirituality of aging inevitably involves preparing for one's death. A few years ago at Thanksgiving dinner, my father's first cousin—a man my father's age, about sixty—pushed back from the table, full from his Derby Pie and turkey stuffing, headed to the front door, and collapsed. Cousin Gene, it turned out, was in good health—perhaps he collapsed because he'd eaten too much, perhaps he'd simply been exhausted. But in the moments before the doctors declared Gene fit and fine, a very particular look passed over the faces of my father and uncle. They were both imagining that Gene had had a stroke, which seems to be the Angel of Death's favorite tool when it comes to the Winner family. As my sister Leanne described it, "You could see them thinking, *It's started. Our generation just began to die.*"

The very old often say they have made their peace with death, but few of us have that equanimity at thirty or forty or fifty. The very process of making peace is part of the opportunity that aging affords.

It is worth noting that through the nineteenth century, Americans' idea of a good death was one in which you lingered; you grew ill and knew death was imminent and thus you had time to settle accounts, with your debtors and your family and also your Maker. It is only in this last century that Americans have wished to be caught unawares in our sleep, looking for a death that is quick and painless and, also, a death for which we cannot prepare.

Christianity and Judaism both offer narratives that make sense of death, but they do not explain it away. No one who has encountered death can deny that it is disordered. Scripture understands that disordering as a result—a punishment—of the Fall. And the Christian narrative tells us that Jesus comes to rectify the Fall, to restore the order of Creation, to triumph over death. In Paul's magnificent summary, "Just as sin entered the world through one man, and death through sin, and in this way death came to all men . . . so also the result of one act of righteousness [the Incarnation, death and Resurrection of Christ] was justification that brings life for all men." This isn't a papering over. This doesn't mean that faithful Christians aren't scared of death—of course we are. In her book *Getting Over Getting Older,* Letty Cottin Pogrebin titles one chapter "Death and the Future—Not Necessarily in That Order." But for those of us who profess resurrection of the dead, we know that is indeed the necessary order.

In the 1970s, an anthropologist named Barbara Myerhoff spent several years studying an elderly Jewish community in Venice, California. Her book *Number Our Days* depicts men and women who were scraping by on small fixed incomes; many were in declining health; many died before Myerhoff's book was published. But the elderly people Myerhoff chronicled were also independent, resilient, imaginative, and often happy. In Myerhoff's words, they "participat[ed] . . . in an active social life and enjoy[ed] a culture built out of a cherished common past."

Did the old Jews in Venice, California, do aging so well because of the textual imperatives of rabbinic Judaism? Not directly. What set them apart was that they lived within a community and a tradition that could help them remember who they were. Myerhoff didn't chronicle individual Jews living atomized lives on the West Coast; the elderly at Aliyah Senior Citizens' Center came together regularly for shared meals, classes in Jewish literature, the occasional prayer service. They spoke together in Yiddish and traded tales about life in Europe before the Holocaust. They raised money for Israeli charities. They celebrated birthdays and mourned deaths.

Christians, it seems to me, have the resources to organize their communal lives, and in particular the lives of elderly Christians, in a similar way. Community is, of course, central to Christianity at every life stage—after all, the very life of the Triune God tells us that we are persons only when we are in communion with one another. But community is especially important at certain life stages. Consider teenagers. Adolescence is all about the articulation of identity, and parents who want to form their teenagers will see to it that they are in communities— schools, churches, families, friendships— that can do the work of reminding them who they are.

So too with the elderly. When our memories fail, it is our community that can tell us who we are. If, like both of my grandmothers, we are lucky enough to have lived in the same town our whole adult lives, the community can remember our personal specific life histories. But even if we pick up and move across the country to be near our kids or to retire somewhere sunny and warm, the community of the church can remind us of our identity in Christ.

Scripture suggests that memory happens in community. When Israel requires some- thing of God, the people of Israel remind God of their relationship, telling and retelling Him stories of the promises He made to Israel, the things He did for His people in past genera- tions. As Kathleen Fischer has explained, faith communities add "an essential dimension to our remembering. In faith we not only gather our memories; we recollect our lives before God. Our stories then take on . . . meaning as a part of a larger story that redeems and embraces them."

———— ∞∞∞ ————

Griff's grandfather, Granddaddy Gatewood, will tell you that his wife, who died a few years ago, was a beautiful woman, but he does not remember many of the details of their life together, or even of his life last week.

This loss of memory is, of course, hard and sad and bitter for everyone who knows him. But it is eased a bit because Dr. Gatewood lives in a community that remembers for him, that can tell the stories of being Dr. Gatewood that even the man himself has forgotten.

A few years ago, Dr. Gatewood told Griff that he loved a woman I'll call Miss B., who has the funkiest glasses in the South, and whom he has known forever, though he cannot recall her name. One might, in a bittersweet sort of way, laugh and wonder at that romantic claim—I did, when Griff told me the story. I wondered how someone could be in love with a woman whose name he could not remember.

But when I went to Americus and saw Dr. Gatewood and Miss B. together, his love for her made sense. Miss B., I'm sure, is interesting and charming in her own right, but she is also a part of the community that remembers Dr. Gatewood, and she remembers many of the things he would remember if he could. His love for her makes sense because it is a love played out against this backdrop: They have loved the same things and people their whole adult lives, and Miss B. remembers who Dr. Gatewood is.

<hr />

Contemporary America has done a pretty good job of marking some of the happier milestones of aging. We throw champagned and smiling parties for our parents' golden wedding anniversaries, and we roast our colleagues when they retire. What we have failed to mark are the harder places of aging—the day you sell your house and move into a retirement apartment or nursing home, the day you finally turn in your driver's license, the day you buy a wheelchair.

A few weeks ago, Lucy and I went to purchase, finally, a hearing aid for her old and imperfect ears. I had tried to come up with some ritual to mark this moment, but everything I could think of seemed hokey and contrived. (For example, I considered making a grand lunch of delicious cream sauce over orecchiette, the pasta whose name translates as "little ears.") In the end, we skipped the pasta and, after procuring the hearing aid, went to Continental Divide for margaritas instead. We toasted Giovanni Battista Porta, the sixteenth-century Neapolitan chemist and alchemist often credited with inventing the hearing aid.

Days later I ask Lucy whether she's adjusted to her new contraption. She says she's thrilled with it. "I can hear all sorts of details that had been lost in an indistinct buzz and mush," she says, but she also says that for an hour every morning, she turns her hearing aid off. "This is like closing your eyes when you pray," she says. "To help yourself concentrate in prayer, you close your eyes and render yourself temporarily blind, but only those of us with lousy hearing and top-of-the-line hearing aids have the option of temporarily rendering ourselves deaf." She says that in the silence, or buzz, or mush, worldly noises do not distract her from the clear voice of God.

nine

hadlakat nerot
candle-lighting

I usually pooh-pooh anything that seems too trendy, but lately I've been filling my house with candles. Shaped like stars, crescents, or old-fashioned columns; blue, yellow, cranberry, glittery, striped; and of course scented: Jumping Jasmine and Lemonberry Meringue are my two most recent purchases, not to mention the Christmas Cookiedough candles I procured back in December.

I'm not alone in my candle fetish. "Candles [are] everywhere," a recent article in the *Miami Herald* declared, "and I mean *everywhere.*" Americans, apparently, spend more than two billion dollars a year on candles. And what is one of the hottest spots of the candlestick trade? Spirituality sales.

Candles are part of bedside altars, sun-porch shrines, and meditation gardens. We sniff up all those scents not because we like aroma, but because we like aromatherapy. We are buying candles not just because of the romance they promise, but because they are good for the soul.

Even though—or perhaps because—literal illumination is as easy as, well, the flip of a switch, there's something remarkable about a candle. There seems to be no surer way to sacralize time or space than lighting a candle, and no quieter quiet than the silence of candlelight. Candles are peaceful, and transfixing, and also ancient. The candle craze may be recent, but New Agers aren't the first to figure out that candles can calm and still and center and sanctify. Candle making as we know it didn't begin until the twelfth century.

———— ◦◦◦ ————

So candles per se are not found in Hebrew Scripture—the ancient children of Israel first spoke of oil lamps and torches, and only eventually adopted paraffin and palm oil and tallow. Candles are everywhere in contemporary Judaism. In the synagogue, in front of the cabinet that holds the Torah scrolls, burns the *ner tamid*, the eternal light, which is never allowed to be extinguished. Memorial candles commemorate the dead. Chanukah is marked by the nightly lighting of an eight-branched candelabrum, the *menorah*.

And candles bracket the Jewish Sabbath. On Friday evening, women usher the Sabbath into their homes by lighting two candles. This is the moment when the hectic, last-minute Shabbat preparations become last week's work, and the peace of the Sabbath begins. After you light the candles, you close your eyes and beckon the light toward you three times with your hands, almost like you are drawing water from a basin to your face. There is something both meditative and practical about drawing the candlelight and the Sabbath stillness into yourself with your hands.

Candles mark the end of the Sabbath as well. In the ceremony called *havdalah*—

which literally means "separation," in this case the separation between Sabbath and week—one lights a multi-wicked, braided candle. The sages explain the origins of the *havdalah* candle with a story. Adam was frightened at the end of the first Shabbat, and God gave him the flickering *havdalah* candle as a promise that Shabbat would return. And each week, the confidence of the *havdalah* candle helps the transition from Sabbath to week; at the end of Shabbat, as the busyness of the work week begins, there is something reassuring in that last tranquil moment of candlelight. This promised quiet is part of what I am looking for when I light my Lemonberry Meringue and set it on the edge of my bathtub. Candles seem to create peace. You don't find candles lit in frenetic houses; you find them lit in houses where people are trying to pay attention.

Christian homes are not typically as candle-filled as Jewish homes. We Christians do not traditionally light candles to usher in the Sabbath or memorialize the dead. But in our communal home, the church, we do indeed have candles, at almost every turn of the liturgical year. We begin during Advent, the month before Christmas, during which we prepare to celebrate both Jesus' coming to earth in Bethlehem and His coming again in glory. We make Advent wreaths out of seasonal greens and four candles. Each week we light one more candle, edging closer out of the darkness of unredemption and toward the light of Jesus' coming.

This is, historically, a church ritual, but more and more people are making Advent wreaths for their homes, too. My five-year-old friend Henry insisted last year that his mother make an Advent wreath. When she asked why he wanted one so very much, he said he wanted something like Chanukah. (A strange cultural reversal in a country that has so long been home to Jewish children wanting something like Christmas.) Griff, my beau, made an Advent wreath this year out of greens he plucked from a friend's yard. We put the wreath on his kitchen table and lit the candles before dinner, the wreath both making a candlelit date out of an ordinary meal and helping us live into a liturgical season so easily overshadowed by Santa Claus lists and shopping trips and cookie exchanges.

Advent and Christmas, in their wintery dark, are not the only liturgical moments for candles. The Advent wreath is really something of a dress rehearsal for the Paschal, or Easter, candle. In the Paschal candle, which Christians have been lighting since at least the sixth century, we see that candlelight symbolizes not only, as at Advent, Christ's Incarnation, but also His Resurrection. Here the flame points to the light of Christ's Resurrection triumphing over the darkness of death. The candle is lit in the dark of the nighttime Easter Vigil, and as it is processed through the church, the people sing this simple chant: "The light of Christ. Thanks be to God."

There is a story in the Talmud about Rabbi Jose. Rabbi Jose says he had studied and studied but was never able to understand a particular verse in Deuteronomy 28: "And you shall grope at noonday as the blind man gropes in pitch-black darkness." *Why,* Rabbi Jose wondered, *would a blind man grope specifically in the darkness? What difference does it make to him whether it is dark or light?* While musing on this problem one (pitch-black) night, Rabbi Jose came across a blind man walking with a torch. "Why," Rabbi Jose asked the man, "do you carry that torch? With or without it, you cannot see a thing!" "True enough," said the blind man, "but as long as I carry this torch, other people can see me."

Rabbi Michael Strassfeld tells that story when teaching about Chanukah. The light of the *menorah*, he says, "lets us see each other and thereby enables us to help each other on our journeys. Despite the darkness, in [the Chanukah candles'] light we can see clearly from one end of [the] world to the other."

Rabbi Strassfeld, of course, is not speaking to the church, but I find in his words a helpful insight into one of Christendom's most persistent metaphors for Jesus: He is, we say, the light of the world. He is the way, to borrow Rabbi Strassfeld's phrase, that we can see clearly from one end of the world to the other.

———— ⟨∞⟩ ————

In Judaism, candle-lighting has historically been associated with women. (The *Miami Herald* article suggests that nothing has changed: "Candles have failed to cross the gender gap. They're a chick thing.") The Talmud names kindling the Sabbath lights as one of three commandments specifically incumbent upon women—the other two are baking *challah* and observing the laws that govern sexual relations between husband and wife.

Kindling is not all women do with candles. There is an old Jewish folk custom called "the laying of wicks," observed during the autumnal season of Rosh Hashanah and Yom Kippur (the new year and the Day of Atonement). Sometime during this holy season, women walked through cemeteries, measuring the gravestones with candlewick and reciting special prayers. On the night before Yom Kippur, they made candles from these wicks, Shabbat candles to be lit by those still living and memorial candles to be lit in honor of those who were dead. The candles, once made and lighted, were thought to awaken the dead, who would in turn intercede with God on behalf of the living. One famous prayer for the laying of wicks calls upon Adam and Eve to "rectify the sin by which they brought death to the world."

This is a somewhat obscure practice, to be sure, but one year in a fit of enthusiasm for the esoteric, my friend Shelby and I decided to head to a graveyard and measure some graves. It was only just past Yom Kippur, and Shelby had just read a scholarly article about the history of the laying of wicks. It seemed a good activity for two Jewish college girls. We pulled on rubber boots and packed raisins and other snacks and set off with our prayers and our lengths of candlewick. Once we got there, we didn't do much measuring. ("Did your article explain how exactly to do this measuring?" I asked Shelby. "Not really," she allowed.) But we did say the prayers, and we did eat our raisins, and Shelby told me about her grandmother, who was buried in that very cemetery.

We never made the candles, either; eventually Shelby braided the wick into thick, ropey jewelry, reminiscent of the bracelets teenaged girls make at summer camp.

Shelby has since entered rabbinical school, and one autumn weekend I go visit her in New York. We decide, finally, to make some candles. When our great-grandmothers made them on the frontier, the task must have been simpler; Shelby lists all the necessary implements, and I know they did not have all this stuff in the Nebraska territory in the nineteenth century: scissors and a hammer and a jiffy wicker (I do not know what this is) and a dash of Kemamide (ditto) and wax, of course, and a candle mold. I am intimidated. This is perhaps not worth the effort. Perhaps I should take myself down to Ye Olde Candle Shoppe and purchase one of those brown candles with coffee beans stuck (glued? Kemamided?) onto the side. But we get started. Shelby lends me her wicking needle, and tells me that Kemamide is a powder that helps candles come lose from their molds. ("Think bundt cakes," she says. "Kemamide is like the grease that prevents the cake from sticking in clumps on the inside of the pan.")

We melt the wax, and prepare the wick, and thread said wick through the mold, and at the end we have a candle. Eight of them, actually. I take them home. I light them at my bathroom sink, and at the kitchen counter, and on the old green desk, and by my bed. I like to keep them lit whenever I am home. Even when I am just lighting two thin tapers over dinner, I like to think about the light of Christ rectifying the sin by which came death to the world. *The Light of Christ,* I sometimes say to myself. *Thanks be to God.*

kiddushin ten
weddings

It is not rare, when you're in your mid-twenties, to be invited to three weddings in a single weekend. This weekend was one of those. I'd already declined an invitation to the gala bash (881 closest friends on the invite list) in Denver, but the other two weddings were in New York, spaced such that I could attend them both. Couple A was married on Saturday on a horse farm just upstate. Couple B was married on Sunday at a hotel in Manhattan. Couple A was Episcopalian. Couple B was Jewish. Both weddings were beautiful. At both, I toasted my friends with champagne, and flirted with men I'd never met before, and danced to Tony Bennett songs. At both weddings, the attendants wore dresses the color of vegetables, and the brides wore tulle. At both, I cried.

And yet, the weddings could not have been more different.

I love the solemn dignity of Christian weddings. I love the wedding rite of the Book of Common Prayer. I love Thomas Cranmer's rhythmic and bawdy 1549 language: "With this ring, I thee wed, . . . with my body, I thee worship." I love it when Christian brides and grooms choose the old language and *pledge their troth,* even though I always have to go home and look up *troth* in the dictionary. (*Troth,* n., "one's pledged fidelity," so actually pledging one's troth is something of a redundancy.)

But Jewish weddings are wonderful in their overt, undeniable joy. At Jewish weddings, everyone sings and dances and is almost raucous. My friend Shelby once remarked that Jewish weddings are just more fun than Christian weddings, and, on the whole, I have to agree.

The differences, though, are not merely aesthetic, Cranmer vs. klezmer or Hebrew instead of antique English. The ceremonies

are different because the communities'
understandings of marriage are different,
and there is truth in each.

—⚬⚬⚬—

I admit that this is one of the places the
Christian church has me forever: The way
Christians make marriages makes sense to
me. Christian wedding vows insist that
marriage is a covenant, not a contract; that if
marriage is not inviolable, divorce is still
only to be undertaken in the rarest possible
circumstances; that God is specially present
at the Christian ceremony of marriage, and it
is His presence that makes possible the
astounding promises people promise; that
marriage is, to use church-speak, sacramental.

Here is where Jewish and Christian
theories of marriage conflict. The vows in a
Jewish wedding ceremony are simple. As the
groom puts the ring on the bride's finger, he
says, "Behold, you are consecrated to me
according to the laws of Moses and Israel."
Then comes the reading of the *ketubah*, a
contract dating at least to the second century

CE. The traditional version names the date and place of the wedding, and then details the monetary settlement the groom will owe the bride in case of divorce. (In recent years, liberal Jews have written any number of alternate *ketubot*.) I remember, once upon a time, thinking this was a very grave but profound and insightful way to begin a marriage, this recognition of the possibility of failure. I now feel discomfited when sitting through this segment of Jewish weddings, when it is laid bare that I am indeed watching a contractual agreement, not a sacramental covenant; and I have to remind myself that Hebrew Scripture, the Old Testament, permits divorce under many circumstances. It is only with Jesus' stern words to the Pharisees that divorce became a very occasional exception to the ever more normative lifelong marriage.

In this nuptial particular, I feel that Christianity tells the best story. But theology, I realize, is different from sociology, and the statistics—which show evangelical Christians divorcing at a rate just slightly higher than that of the rest of America—suggest that however perfect in theory, something about Christian marriage-making (or, at least, Christian marriage-keeping) does not work. And here is where Jewish nuptials, depressing *ketubah* notwithstanding, are wise. If the *ketubah* makes my shoulders tense up, everything that surrounds the *ketubah* makes good sense. I wish we could import some of it to the church.

The visible symbols and icons of Jewish weddings are familiar. A Jewish couple is married under a *chuppah*, a four-cornered canopy, often made from cloth, sometimes extravagantly made of flowers. The *chuppah* symbolizes the roof of the home the couple will make together, and also the intimate fabric of their bedcovers, and also the sure protection of God's love.

Under the *chuppah*, after the exchange of rings and the reading of the *ketubah* and the pronouncing of blessings, comes the famous breaking of glass—the groom crushes a goblet (wrapped in a packet or bag, of course) under his feet. The broken glass warns of the frailty of marriage; it also recalls the destruction of the Temple in Jerusalem, a somber moment of Jewish history that should be remembered at even the most joyous occasions. Another interpretation holds that the loud crunch of the glass scares off any demons who might have been hanging around, plotting to trip up the wedding party. Still another holds that the breaking glass foreshadows the consummation of marriage.

Yet while the broken glass and the bold *chuppah* are memorable accoutrements of Jewish weddings, the most important things happen after, not under, the *chuppah*.

At the heart of weddings—because also at the heart of marriage—is the balance between privacy and community. Marriage, to be sure, is an intimate matter, the making of a partnership that knits two people together in secret and inside ways (just consider what Adam says of Eve: "bone of my bones and flesh of my flesh.") But it is a pernicious myth of modernity that marriage is merely private: Marriage is also a community endeavor. It is your friends and family who help you stay straight and true when your marriage feels too crooked or curvy. It is your sister or best friend or bridesmaid who can remind you why you ever married him in the first place. It is the neighbor or confidant who is just outside the thing who can sometimes tell you the truth about it.

This is the balance the Jewish wedding strikes exactly right. To see the balance, one must look at two end pieces of the Jewish wedding ceremony: *yichud* and *sheva brachot*. *Yichud* and *sheva brachot* both come after the ceremony—after the *chuppah* and the *ketubah* and the breaking of glass—but together they get at the essence of marriage-making.

Yichud is onomatopoeic. It is a hushed, whispered word, and it means "privacy." *Yichud*, privacy, is forbidden to the (Orthodox) Jewish couple before they are married. Until nuptials, the door must be kept open, there must be a chaperone—no sex, no impropriety, no aloneness. And so the very first thing he and she do after that glass is broken is escape off for a few minutes of *yichud*, a few minutes of aloneness, behind a closed door. In earlier eras, the marriage was actually consummated in the *yichud* room. Nowadays, there's just a good bit of smooching. If the couple is among the most devout Jews, those who observe the laws that require unmarried couples to have no physical contact at all, then there in the *yichud* room a single peck on the cheek is a spark-sending, faint-inducing big deal. I remember well the first Orthodox Jewish wedding I attended. When the bride and groom came out of the *yichud* room, they simply could not stop holding hands. It was the first time their hands had ever touched.

That coming out of the *yichud* room is the very point, the place where privacy gives way to community. As much as the hand-holding couple wanted to be alone, to stay immersed in alone for hours on end, they came back to their friends, to the neighbors and relatives who will uphold them in their new strange life together.

For observant Jews, there is no honey-moon, at least not immediately. The so-called "laws of family purity"—the laws that dictate when married couples may and may not have sex—require seven days of abstinence after The Wedding Night. And, really, what is the point of going on a honeymoon if you have to sleep in separate beds?

Instead of honeymooning, the newly-weds attend seven nights of parties in their honor. These parties are called the *sheva brachot*, after the "seven blessings" recited at each post-wedding bash. Intended to distract husband and wife from one another's sexual charms, these parties can range from a casual pizza get-together to the most formal champagne and caviar. (An added social plus: one can invite to the *sheva brachot* friends and acquaintances who didn't make it onto the wedding guest list.)

Whether or not these fetes work as anti-aphrodisiacs is anyone's guess. What they do—not unlike the rites after a funeral—is push married couples into their community. Marriage, after all, is not just a change in individual circumstances. The new husband and wife will relate differently to one another, to be sure, but they will also engage the community differently, and night after night of festivities smooth that strange transition for everyone involved. Here are the *sheva brachot*, seven nightly reminders that marriage is a group project, a communal commitment.

The great surprise of the week (at least, I am letting him think it was a surprise) is that Griff asked me to marry him. So now I find that all my theoretical musings about weddings suddenly become less theoretical.

I am already amazed at all the details, and how everyone has an opinion about which caterers I should call, and how easy it is to forget about marriage and think only about the wedding.

So far, I've gotten one piece of wedding advice that seems very sound. Our friends the Willards told us to pick one priority, one thing that we care about, and make that one thing as perfect as possible, and let everything else fall into place behind it. The photography? The reception venue? The dress?

I was assured I was marrying the right person when Griff said, without missing a beat, that the most important thing to him was somehow creating community at our wedding. (Where did he learn that, I wonder, since he didn't grow up Jewish?)

And so that is what we are trying to do. We are trying to invite people who are part of our pasts and presents. We will plan a weekend full of activities where our friends from the far-flung corners of the globe can, at least a little bit, get to know one another. And then, if we manage not to split up over questions of menu and music and boutonnières, we will one evening, some months from now, stand at the front of Christ Church while our priest asks our gathered community "Will all of you witnessing these promises do all in your power to uphold these two persons in their marriage?" And our community will answer, "We will."

eleven
mezuzot
doorposts

When I was twelve, a friend from the synagogue gave me a *mezuzah*: a small roll of parchment tucked inside a glass tube. The glass was gauzy, like translucent Tiffany glass, streaked with summer colors: pink, and green, and purple. At the top and bottom of the tube, there were tiny holes made for tiny nails, and I took the *mezuzah* home, and said the blessing that praises the God who has commanded us to affix the *mezuzah*, and nailed it to the doorframe outside my bedroom.

The practice of affixing a *mezuzah* to one's door finds it's origin in a passage from Deuteronomy: "You shall love the LORD your God with all your heart and with all your soul and with all your might. These words, which I am commanding you today, shall be on your heart. . . . You shall write them on the doorposts of your house and on your gates."

You shall write them on the doorposts of your house: In obedience to that verse, Jews purchase special tiny scrolls of parchment on which are calligraphied fifteen verses from the sixth and eleventh chapters of Deuteronomy (the very verses in which the command to *inscribe them on your doorposts* is found). The parchment is hidden inside a decorative case or tube. Both the parchment itself and the plastic or ceramic or silver or wooden case are called a *mezuzah* (the plural is *mezuzot*). These are the boxes you see on the doors outside Jewish homes. You'll find them inside, too, on the doorposts to any room in which people live: bedrooms, kitchens, drawing rooms—every room, really, other than bathrooms and stables.

In college (yes, one is commanded to hang a *mezuzah* on one's college dorm room doorpost—anywhere one will be living longer than a month), I purchased a new *mezuzah*. You purchase the scroll itself, generally, at a Judaica shop, but you can find the cases anywhere. I bought mine, a small silver case with delicate filigree, at an art gallery in Greenwich Village.

Jews got serious about the business of decorating *mezuzah* cases in the eighteenth or nineteenth century. There is an elaborate North African *mezuzah* case that dates to sometime in the 1700s, and by the nineteenth century Jews in Russia, eastern Europe, and Morocco were shaping *mezuzah* cases out of silver, creating miniature arks and fish and other pretty symbols in which to house their slices of parchment. Today one can find *mezuzah* cases made of pewter, clay, wood, crystal, even hammered gold. Creative craftsy types can make their own *mezuzot*; outside my friend Perry's bedroom is a *mezuzah* made from a pink plastic toothbrush case.

The younger set can purchase a Snoopy *mezuzah*, a Braves *mezuzah* in the shape of a baseball bat, a dinosaur *mezuzah* painted in Barney-purple. The hard-nosed toy-shopper can find miniature *mezuzot* made for dollhouses. (I've even heard there are special tiny *mezuzot* for Barbie to use, but I've never seen one, nor do I recall reading that the WASPish Mattel doll converted to Judaism.)

Is consumer culture infecting the *mezuzah*? Sure. But there is something grand to the dressing up of the simple *mezuzah*— it is consonant with the underlying Jewish attitude toward beauty. One should, whenever possible, beautify one's commandments. Why have a plain Jane *mezuzah* when one can affix works of art to one's doorposts?

From Snoopy to silver filigree, almost every *mezuzah* case is decorated with the Hebrew letter *shin*:‫ש‬. This three-pronged letter, which looks a little like the top of a pitchfork, begins the *Shema*, the Jewish prayer, found in Deuteronomy 6:4, that declares the oneness of God: *Hear, O Israel, the LORD our God, the LORD is one.* This prayer, repeated over and over in the Jewish liturgy, is meant to be the last thing a Jew says before dying. It is included in the verses copied onto the *mezuzah* parchment. The *mezuzah* case, then, is not just a decorative item. It is also a restatement of the essence of Jewish faith.

Shin is also the first letter of the word *shalom*, peace. If having a *mezuzah* on one's door does not necessarily make one's home a peaceful refuge from the hostile world, it does serve as a reminder: a reminder of *shalom bayit,* peace in the home, an ideal toward which every Jewish home is meant to strive. Once, when my college roomie and I were duking it out over the dishes (in the sink) and the bathtub (filthy) and the phone (ringing much too late at night), the *mezuzah* squelched our screaming. In the middle of railing about the long hair destined to clog our bathtub pipes, my roommate walked to our bedroom door and tapped on the front of the *mezuzah*, and we smiled and laughed and breathed deeply and started to wash the dishes. Little *mezuzah* reminders don't work miracles, of course, but sometimes they help the fights simmer down and the dishes get clean.

The *shin* that decorates a *mezuzah* case also stands for the phrase *Shomer daltot*

Yisrael, "guardian of the doors of Israel." And, indeed, since at least the Middle Ages, many Jews have thought of the *mezuzah* as an amulet, a charm-working talisman that would keep the demons and evil spirits away. The rabbis have not been overly fond of that folk belief, but even they have allowed that a *mezuzah*, insofar as it is a small physical reminder of God's power and presence, does keep us from harm's way. According to the Talmud, the Jew who wears phylacteries on his arm and fringed *tzitzit* on his garments and affixes a *mezuzah* to his door, "is sure not to sin because he has many reminders of God; and these reminders are the very guardian angels who protect him from sinning."

Finally, the *shin* that decorates *mezuzah* cases is also the letter that begins the word *shofar*. A *shofar* is a ram's horn, and in synagogues, the *shofar* is blown like a trumpet during the most sacred days of the Jewish year, the High Holy Days of Rosh Hashanah and Yom Kippur, the new year and the Day of Atonement. The lowing song of the *shofar* is both a call to atone and a proclamation of faith. The *mezuzah*, too, which interrupts the smooth line of the doorframe and juts into your line of vision, is a proclamation. A *mezuzah*—like Chanukah *menorahs,* which Jews are enjoined not only to light, but to set in their windows—is a real, visible, public witness, a declaration to anyone who would walk by that this is a Jewish home. The people who live here are Jewish, and they are proud of it.

That proclamation is more noticeable here in Charlottesville than in New York. Manhattan is home to such a sizable Jewish community that after a while one doesn't really notice the *mezuzot.* In Charlottesville, a *mezuzah* is a rarer thing. My friend Vanessa lives on St. Anne's Lane, and I can never remember her house number, but whenever I go to visit, I know her house because the *mezuzah* marks it.

Perhaps the most startling Charlottesville *mezuzah* is that of Kevin Hechtkopf. Kevin is the president of Hillel (the campus Jewish organization) here at the University of Virginia, and he lives on the Lawn, the architectural and historical heart of the entire university. Kevin, now in his final year at UVA, had not bothered with *mezuzot* during his first three years of college. But an iridescent black *mezuzah* now hangs outside his room on the widely trafficked Lawn. Kevin's *mezuzah* is spied daily by professors, administrators, students, even sometimes a governor or visiting dignitary. Here on the grounds of the college designed by the same Thomas Jefferson who drafted Virginia's Bill of Religious Toleration, Kevin's *mezuzah* is a proclamation. It says, in his words, that "you can be Jewish at UVA—you don't have to hide it."

———— ∞ ————

Years ago, I gave away my delicate silver and glass *mezuzot*. There are no Christian *mezuzot*; I don't even have a Christian fish pasted to the bumper of my car. I have filled my apartment with crosses and old church fans and Crucifixion scenes done in Indian batik. These objects decorate. Like churchly stained-glass windows, they tell stories. They help me remember. They are still not *mezuzot*, though. They do not always ask what I want a Christian home to be like. They do not proclaim to anyone who might pass by that this home is a Christian home.

About two years ago, my friend Bobby and I were walking up Broadway. We saw, on the sidewalk, an old door someone was discarding. "Hey look," I said, "there's a sign on this door." And, indeed, taped to the front of the lonesome sidewalk door was a sign the size of a postcard with a quotation from Psalm 121: "The Lord shall preserve thy going out and thy coming in from this time forth, and even for evermore." The small print on the bottom told me the sign had been produced by the Life-Study Fellowship in Noroton, Connecticut. Someone, perhaps the guy who was getting rid of the door, had scribbled on the sign *Keep home safe thank God.* The handwriting was shaky, that of a child or a ninety-year-old.

"Look at this sign," I said to Bobby, marveling.

"Do you want it?" Bobby asked.

"Why, yes, I do," I said. And I pried the little sign off the door and put it in my purse.

I used to keep it propped up on my dresser, mixed in with a photo of my father, a bakelite compact I bought on eBay, and an old wooden glove box that I keep full of forget-me-nots. While helping me clean for a party, my friend Molly said, "Lauren, why don't you put this sign up on your door?" *Good thinking,* I thought. I took the sign and located a roll of tape and began to affix it to my bedroom door. "No," Molly said, "your front door."

I inhaled sharply. "But, Molly," I said, "if I do that, the whole world will know I'm a Christian." Molly looked at me and wiggled her eyebrows. There it was, my old discomfort with what we Christians call witnessing, my ever-present hesitation to proclaim the gospel, my deep-seated suspicion that Christianity is fine as long as it's private.

Molly cleared her throat. She tapped her fingers on the top of my dresser. "Hmmm," I said. (Did I mention this was a St. Lucia Day party, and that I'd spent all afternoon trying to make the cardamom-and saffron-filled St. Lucia Day buns, and that only Christian nerds newly infatuated with the saints' days do such things?) "Right," I said, and I went to the front door and taped up the small rectangular sign from the Life-Study Fellowship.

It is not quite a *mezuzah*. Hanging up a sign one found while waltzing down Broadway is not quite the same as fulfilling a no-nonsense commandment to inscribe the doorposts of your house. But this sign accomplishes some of the same space and memory work of *mezuzot*.

Every time I come home I see the sign, and I remember that I claim to actually believe in this God who will preserve my going out and coming in, and I remember that this home is supposed to be a Christian home. It is to be a home into which I invite strangers, and in which I organize my time through prayers, and in which I do work that might somehow infinitesimally advance the kingdom of God.

And when I walk in and out of my apartment and see the psalmist sign, I also remember the proclamation that I am making to others: the sign tells you that I am a person who is trying to be a Christian, and in telling that to you, I am inviting you to hold me to it.

It is just the doorway, but this is the beginning of making Christian space out of an ordinary apartment.

acknowledgments

I am grateful to those who read drafts of many of these chapters: Molly Bosscher Davis, Kristine Harmon, Charles Marsh, Jenny McBride, Erika Meitner, Vanessa Ochs, Professor Marvin R. Wilson, Felicia Wu Song, Beth Bogard Vander Wel, Brian Vander Wel, and my students at the Charlottesville Writing Center

Special thanks to Griff Gatewood, who worked his way through many drafts, and who helped me keep body and soul together during a few hectic writing weeks; and to Shani Offen, old friend and peerless *dikduk* point girl; and to Mary E. Lyons, for sharp eyes and pencils, and hospitality. Amanda Beer, proprietor of Charlottesville's remarkable Splintered Light bookstore, provided encouragement and, of course, books.

Thanks to Carol Mann, heroic agent and confidante, and to the good folks at Paraclete, most especially Lil Copan, for patience and fortitude (and all the other virtues besides).

notes

introduction

pp.ix–x. *This* midrash *explains a curious turn of phrase in Exodus 24.* Exodus 24:7 Talmud, Masechet Shabbat 88a.

p.xi. *Christian tradition has developed a wealth of practices.* . . . The most influential recent book on Christian spiritual practice is Richard J. Foster, *Celebration of Discipline: The Path to Spiritual Growth* (San Francisco: Harper and Row, 1978).

p.xii. "Christ, and him crucified."
1 Corinthians 2:2.

one
shabbat / sabbath

pp.1–2. *"On Friday afternoon . . . Shabbat is a meditation of unbelievable beauty."*
Nan Fink, *Stranger in the Midst: A Memoir of Spiritual Discovery* (New York: Basic Books, 1997), 95–96.

p.4. *"Remember the Sabbath day and keep it holy."*
Exodus 20:8.

p.4. *"observe the Sabbath day and keep it holy."*
Deuteronomy 5:12.

p.4. *"come to worship before me."*
Isaiah 66:23.

p.5. *"You shall not . . . sojourner who dwells among you."*
Exodus 20:10 and Deuteronomy 5:14.

pp.6–7. *"What happens . . . it is God's world."*
Lis Harris, *Holy Days: The World of a Hasidic Family* (New York: Touchstone Books, 1995), 68–69.

pp.9–10. *"Therefore do not let anyone judge you . . . the reality, however, is found in Christ."*
Col 2: 16–17 NIV.

p.10. *"the Sabbath was made for man, not man for the Sabbath."*
Mark 2:27 NIV.

p.11. *"Six days shall you labor and do all your work. But the seventh day is a sabbath to the LORD your God."*
Exodus 20:9–10 and Deuteronomy 5:13–14.

p.12. *"Good Sabbaths make good Christians."*
Dorothy Bass, "Keeping Sabbath," in Dorothy Bass, ed., *Practicing Our Faith: A Way of Life for a Searching People* (San Francisco: Jossey–Bass, 1997), 83–88.

pp.12–13. *"Under the New Testament . . . Retire to rest betimes."*
Johann Friedrich Starck, *Daily Handbook for Days of Joy and Sorrow,* excerpted in Peter C. Erb, *Pietists: Selected Writings* (New York: Paulist Press, 1983), 181–82.

two
kashrut / fitting food

pp.15–16. *No shellfish, no pork . . . now it is a meat pot forever.*
This list is inspired by Elizabeth Erlich's wonderful musings on keeping kosher: Elizabeth Erlich, *Miriam's Kitchen: A Memoir* (New York: Viking, 1997), 14–17.

p.16. *"Thou shalt not seethe a kid in his mother's milk."*
Deuteronomy 14:21 KJV.

p.17. *Rabbi Abraham Joshua Heschel observed . . . death (meat) and life (milk).*
Arthur Waskow, *Down-to-Earth Judaism: Food, Money, Sex, and the Rest of Life* (New York: William Morrow, 1997), 78.

pp.19–20. *In the Book of Acts . . . "you must not call profane."*
Acts of the Apostles 10:13, 15.

p.20. *Humanity's first sin was disobedience manifested in a choice about eating.*
Waskow, *Down-to-Earth Judaism,* 17–21.

pp.22–23. *The second chapter of* The Supper of the Lamb . . . *"His present delight."*
Robert Farrar Capon, *The Supper of the Lamb: A Culinary Reflection* (New York: Pocket Books, 1970), 10–11, 15–16. I am grateful to the Reverend Brian Vander Wel for directing my attention to Capon's onion.

p.24. *"Even if you walk or bike . . . some serious gas."*
Barbara Kingsolver, *Small Wonder* (New York: Harper Collins, 2002), 114. Thanks to Mary Lyons for pointing out to me that Edna Lewis and Alice Waters pioneered and popularized the current fascination with seasonal eating.

three
avelut / mourning

p.29. *During these days, mourners are exempt . . . "border on death themselves."*
Margaret Holub, "A Cosmology of Mourning," in Debra Orenstein, ed., *Lifecycles: Jewish Women on Life Passages and Personal Milestones* (Woodstock, VT: Jewish Lights, 1994), 345–46.

p.29–33. *The next demarked days are* shiva *. . . all different pieces of commemorating, remembering, celebrating, and mourning.*
Samuel C. Heilman, *When A Jew Dies: The Ethnography of a Bereaved Son* (Berkeley: University of California Press, 2001), 119–21, 134–35, 159–60, passim.

p.30. *"they sat down with him . . . and no one spoke a word to him."*
Job 2:13 (as quoted in Heilman).

p.35–36. *that the* Kaddish *is a curious mourner's prayer . . . the* Kaddish *is really "a Gloria."*
For the Gloria, see Heilman, 164. The most affecting recent discussion of this topic is Leon Wieseltier, *Kaddish* (New York: Knopf, 1998), 163–65.

pp.38–39. *I have not said* Kaddish *. . . remember my dead.*
This list echoes Wieseltier, 173.

four
hachnassat orchim / hospitality

p.44. *"you were strangers in the land of Egypt."*
Leviticus 19:34 and Exodus 12:49.

p.44. *"Do not be forgetful to entertain strangers; for thereby some have entertained angels unawares."*
Hebrews 13:2 KJV.

p.45. *Rabbi Yochanan insisted that practicing hospitality . . . bowl of soup they did not like.*
"Hospitality," *Encyclopaedia Judaica,* vol. 8 (Jerusalem: Macmillan, 1971), 1030–33.
"Hospitality," *The Jewish Encyclopedia,* vol. 6 (New York: Funk and Wagnalls, 1904), 480–81.

pp.45–47. *Early Christian communities continued these practices of hospitality . . . "by establishing a home . . . for all."*
Amy G. Oden, ed., *And You Welcomed Me: A Sourcebook on Hospitality in Early Christianity* (Nashville: Abingdon Press, 2001), 87, 145–214, passim.

pp.46–47 In the words of one rabbi," . . . *[The] world is one big hospitality inn."*
http://www.aish.com/spirituality/48ways/Way_14_Written_Instructions_For_Living.asp

p.47. *L'Arche and the Catholic Worker houses. . . .*
On practices of hospitality explicitly connected to the poor, see Christine Pohl, *Making Room: Recovering Hospitality as a Christian Tradition* (Grand Rapids, MI: Eerdmans, 1999).

p.51. *"Visitors may be more than guests in our home. . . ."*
Karen Burton Mains, *Open Heart, Open Home: The Hospitable Way to Make Others Feel Welcome & Wanted* (Elgin, IL: David C. Cook, 1976), 21.

five
tefillah / prayer

p.55. *"Jews do offer freely composed prayers . . . commitment to prayer as a discipline."*
Lawrence Hoffman, *The Way into Jewish Prayer* (Woodstock,VT: Jewish Lights, 2000), 19.

p.56. *"flexible standardization of the liturgy so that anyone attending [a] service anywhere in the country could feel at home, understand, and join in."*
http://www.americanbuddhistcongress.org/budlit.html

p.61. *"May those who seek my life be disgraced . . . ."*
Psalm 35:4, 6 NIV.

six
guf / body

p.67. *Christians, it must be admitted, have not told this story very consistently.*
A wonderful recent Christian resource on the body is Lilian Calles Barger, *Eve's Revenge: Women and a Spirituality of the Body* (Grand Rapids, MI: Brazos Press, 2003).

pp.68–71. *"while in the bathroom it is forbidden . . ." "the taste of the Garden of Eden in the meal."*
Yitzhak Buxbaum, *Jewish Spiritual Practices* (New York: Jason Aronson, 1994), 598, 520, 521, 277, 229, 227.

pp.71–72. *"creating in me many orifices . . . stand before You."*
The text of the *asher yatzar* can be found in any Orthodox Jewish prayerbook, and online at http://www.torahzone.com/AsherYatzar.htm.

p.73. *"the Jewish girl must offset . . . the simplest clothes are the most expensive."*
Riv-Ellen Prell, *Fighting to Be Americans: Assimilation and the Trouble Between Jewish Women and Jewish Men* (Boston: Beacon Press, 2000), 49–50. In this paragraph, the language of "caricature" and "pathology" is drawn from Michael Wyschogrod, *The Body of Faith: God and the People of Israel* (New York: The Seabury Press, 1983), 28.

p.73–74. *"for rabbinic Jews, the human being was defined"* . . .
. . . *"soul housed in a body."*
Daniel Boyarin, *Carnal Israel: Reading Sex in Talmudic Culture* (Berkeley: University of California Press, 1993), 5. Boyarin, in this passage and in the rest of his book, makes clear that Hellenistic Jews, like Philo, shared the Pauline perspective, privileging the soul. Here I focus on rabbinic Judaism because it became the dominant, normative Jewish discourse about bodies. See also Peter Brown, *The Body and Society* (New York: Columbia University Press, 1988).

p.76. *our evening bath as an opportunity to ponder and pray into the baptismal covenant.*
Stephanie Paulsell, *Honoring the Body: Meditations on a Christian Practice* (San Francisco: Jossey-Bass, 2002), 49–56.

p.77. *Then there is the matter of suffering.*
For helpful discussion of Christian suffering, see Paulsell, 165–80.

p.79. *"Slowly, slowly,"* she writes, *"MS will teach me to live as a body."*
Nancy Mairs, *Remembering the Bone House: An Erotics of Place and Space* (New York: Harper and Row, 1989), 235.

seven
tzum / fasting

p.85. *And the Gospel of Matthew makes this scary, flat claim: there are demons that "go not out but by prayer and fasting."* Matthew 17:21. Scholars believe this verse is not part of the original Gosple text. You can find it in the footnotes of most annotated study Bibles. It will also be found in the KJV, ASN, and NASB.

p.86. *As journalist Christine Gardner . . . 43,000 member churches.*
Christine J. Gardner, "Hungry for God: Why More and More Christians Are Fasting for Revival," *Christianity Today* (April 5, 1999), 32.

p.87. *In* A Closer Walk, *she describes. . . .*
Catherine Marshall, *A Closer Walk,* excerpted in Richard J. Foster and Emilie Griffin, eds., *Spiritual Classics* (San Francisco: HarperSanFrancisco, 2002), 57–59.

p.90. *"a perfect quieting of all our impulses, fleshly and spiritual."*
St. Thomas Aquinas quoted in E. E. Holmes, *Prayer and Practice, or, "Three Noble Duties"* (London: Longmans, Green, 1911), 110.

eight
hiddur p'nai zaken / aging

p.93. *Once upon a time, the* midrash *says, . . . age spots and gray whiskers.*
Dayle A. Friedman, "Crown Me With Wrinkles and Gray Hair: Examining Traditional Jewish Views of Aging." In Susan Berrin, ed., *A Heart of Wisdom: Making the Jewish Journey From Midlife Through the Elder Years.* (Woodstock, VT: Jewish Lights, 1997), p.5. Genesis Rabbah 65:9.

p.94. *The young are not to contradict anything their elders say . . . in case an older person should enter the room.*
Friedman, 11.

pp.94–95. *A contemporary Jewish poet, Danny Siegel, has also offered a creative reading of the biblical injunctions about the elderly. . . .*
Danny Siegel, "The Mitzvah of Bringing Out the Beauty of Our Elders' Faces," in Berrin, 50–52. *Hiddur p'nai zaken*, the idea of honoring the face of one's elder, derives from Leviticus 19:32. I take my inspiration for the title of this chapter from Danny Siegel.

p.96. *"I don't ever want to be . . . spending time with her."*
Letty Cottin Pogrebin, *Getting Over Getting Older* (New York: Time Warner, 1996), 304–5.

p.98. *He speaks instead of "eldering." . . . or, in another of Reb Zalman's clever infinitives, "to sage."*
Zalman Schacter-Shalomi, *From Age-ing to Sage-ing: A Profound New Vision of Growing Older* (New York: Warner Books, 1997).

p.99. *The Hebrew word* sayvah *. . . the process of setting wrong things right.*
Susan Berrin, ed., *A Heart of Wisdom: Making the Jewish Journey from Mid-Life Through the Elder Years* (Woodstock, VT: Jewish Lights Publishing, 1999) 33–34.

pp.99–100. *In the Middle Ages. . . . It is also about prayer and attention and preparation and God.*
Shulamith Shahar, *Growing Old in the Middle Ages*, trans. Yael Lotan (New York: Routledge, 1997), 54–59.

p.101. *It is worth noting that through the nineteenth century. . . .*
For a history of American attitudes toward death, see Gary
Laderman, *The Sacred Remains: American Attitudes Toward
Death, 1799–1883* (New Haven: Yale University Press, 1999).

p.101–2. *"Just as sin entered the world . . . justification that
brings life for all men."*
Romans 5:12, 18 NIV.

p.102. *Letty Cottin Pogrebin titles one chapter. . . .*
Pogrebin, 299.

p.102. *they "participat[ed] . . . in an active social life and
enjoy[ed] a culture built out of a cherished common past."*
Barbara Myerhoff, *Number Our Days* (New York: E. P.
Dutton, 1978), 217–18.

p.104–5. *As Kathleen Fischer has explained . . ."Our stories
then take on . . . meaning as a part of a larger story that
redeems and embraces them."*
Kathleen Fischer, *Winter Grace: Spirituality and Aging*
(Nashville: Upper Room Books, 1998) 48–49.

p.106–7. *Contemporary America has done a pretty good
job . . . the day you buy a wheelchair.*
Barbara Myerhoff, *Remembered Lives: The Work of Ritual,
Storytelling, and Growing Older* (Ann Arbor: The
University of Michigan Press, 1972).

nine
hadlakat nerot / candle-lighting

p.109 *"Candles [are] everywhere"* . . . *"and I mean* every-
where."
Ana Veciana Suarez, "Waxing Poetic: Electric Light
Doesn't Cut It," *Miami Herald,* December 22, 2002.

pp.110. *Candlemaking as we know it . . . the twelfth century.*
"Candles," *Encyclopaedia Judaica,* vol. 5 (Jerusalem:
Macmillan, 1971), 117–19.

p.111. *After you light the candles, you close your eyes and beckon. . . .*
See Nina Beth Cardin, *The Tapestry of Jewish Time: A Spiritual Guide to Holidays and Life-Cycle Events* (Springfield, NJ: Behrman House, 2000), 39. Cardin explains another reason for covering the eyes before saying the blessing over the candles: "By reciting a blessing before we enjoy the goodness in our lives, we can enhance the experience and sharpen our appreciation of it. For example we recite the blessing over bread before we eat. However, because Shabbat begins when we say the blessing over the candles and it is forbidden to kindle a fire on Shabbat, we light the candles first and then recite the blessing, covering our eyes so that we do not enjoy the Sabbath light until after we have completed the blessing."

p.112. *Adam was frightened at the end of the first Shabbat. . . .*
Midrash Rabbah 11:2.

p.114–15. *There is a story in the Talmud about Rabbi Jose. . . .*
"we can see clearly from one end of [the] world to the other."
Michael Strassfeld, *A Book of Life: Embracing Judaism as a Spiritual Practice* (New York: Schocken Books, 2002), 288.

p.116. *Candles have failed to cross the gender gap. They're a chick thing.*
Suarez, "Waxing Poetic."

p.116–17. *There is an old Jewish folk custom called "the lay-ing of wicks" . . . "rectify the sin by which they brought death to the world."*
Chava Weissler, *Voices of the Matriarchs: Listening to the Prayers of Early Modern Jewish Women* (Boston: Beacon Press, 1999), 133–44.

ten
kiddushin / weddings

p.123. *It is only with Jesus' stern words to the Pharisees. . . .*
For an accessible, cogent discussion of the New Testament on divorce, see Richard Hays, *The Moral Vision of the New Testament: A Contemporary Introduction to New Testament Ethics* (San Francisco: HarperSanFrancisco, 1996), 347–78.

p.125. *"bone of my bones and flesh of my flesh."*
Genesis 2:23 NIV.

eleven
mezuzah / doorposts

p.131–32. *"You shall love the LORD. . . your house and on your gates."*
Deuteronomy 6:5,6,9 NASB.

p.133. *Jews got serious . . . slices of parchment.*
Erika Meitner, "The *Mezuzah*: American Judaism and Constructions of American Sacred Space," unpublished paper in author's possession, 6.

p.136. *"and affixes a* mezuzah *to his door . . . protect him from sinning."*
Talmud, Masechet Menahot, 43b.

Mezuzot are connected to protection in another way as well. They recall the story of the Exodus from Egypt, in which the Israelites marked their doors with slashes of blood. When the Angel of Death came to slay the first-born of every Egyptian family, the Israelites—identified, and protected, by their sanguinary doorpost markings—were spared.

p.137–38. *Perhaps the most startling Charlottesville* mezuzah . . . *"you don't have to hide it."*
Meitner, 12.

glossary of hebrew and yiddish terms

(Terms are Hebrew unless marked as Yiddish.)

Amidah: Central prayer of Jewish services, composed in the fifth century CE.

aninut: State of mourning between death and burial.

asher yatzar: Literally, "who formed"; blessing recited every morning and after one has gone to the bathroom; expresses recognition that bodies are complex and sophisticated systems.

Av: The fifth month in the Jewish calendar. (The ninth of Av is a fast day that commemorates the destruction of the Temple.)

avelut: Entire period of mourning.

bat mitzvah: "Daughter of the commandments"; girl who has reached the age of twelve and becomes obligated to observe all the commandments.

brit milah (often shortened to *bris* or *brit*): Circumcision ceremony at which an eight-day-old boy enters the covenant of Abraham.

challah: Egg bread, often braided, that is traditionally eaten on the Sabbath.

cholent: Stew consisting of meat, potatoes, and beans simmered overnight; typically served on the Sabbath.

chuppah (pl. *chuppot*): Wedding canopy.

fleishig (Yiddish): Consisting of, prepared with, or relating to meat or meat products.

guf: Body.

hachnassat orchim: The welcoming of guests.

hadlakat nerot: Lighting candles.

Hasidic: Relating to Hasidism, a form of mystical Orthodox Judaism that began in the 1700s in Eastern Europe.

havdalah: Literally, "separation"; the ceremony that concludes the Sabbath.

Kaddish: An Aramaic prayer, central to Jewish liturgy, that praises and glorifies God. The "Mourner's Kaddish" is an iteration of the prayer said by those in mourning. Many commentators have pointed out and, indeed, puzzled over the fact that the Mourner's Kaddish does not mention mourning or bereavment, per se. Some of these commentators have suggested that the work of the prayer is not, strictly speaking, to commemorate the dead, but to point the mourner's attention toward God.

kashrut: Jewish dietary laws.

kavannah: Intention that allows one to offer words or deeds as gifts of inner devotion.

ketubah: Marriage contract.

kiddush: Literally, "sanctification"; a benediction sung or recited over a cup of wine to consecrate the Sabbath or a festival.

kiddushin: Literally, "sanctity" or "setting apart"; also used as a synonym for marriage.

Kol asher diber Adonai na'aseh ve-nishma: "All the words that God has spoken, we will do and we will hear"; from Exodus 24.

mezuzah (pl. *mezuzot*): Literally, "doorpost"; small piece of parchment inscribed with the biblical passages Deuteronomy 6:4–9 and 11:13–21. The parchment is rolled up in a container and affixed to a door frame. *Mezuzah* also denotes the container that holds the parchment.

midrash: Literally, "investigation"; stories elaborating on incidents in the Bible to derive a principle of Jewish law or provide a moral lesson.

mikvah: Pool used for purposes of ritual purification.

Mishnah: Collection of rulings and laws under the leadership of Rabbi Judah Hanasi, collected about 210 CE. These had been passed on orally for a number of generations.

mitzvah (pl. *mitzvot*): Commandment; two types are *mitzvot asei* (positive commandments: "Thou shalt") and *mitzvot lo ta'aseh* (prohibitions: "Thou shalt not").

ner tamid: Eternal light; continually burning lamp that was to be placed in the Tent of Meeting and later in the Temple. Found in contemporary synagogues in front of the cabinet that holds the Torah scrolls.

neshamah yeteirah: Literally, "additional soul"; said to embody the height of spiritual happiness created by the Sabbath.

olam haba: The world to come.

Rosh Hashanah: Jewish new year.

seudat havra'ah: Meal of condolence served to mourners on their return from the funeral.

Shabbat: Seventh day of the week; a day of rest.

Shabbat haMalkah: Literally, the Sabbath queen; image of the Sabbath as a queen to be honored and welcomed.

shalom bayit: Peace in the home; harmony between family members.

shechitah: Ritual slaughter of animals that may be eaten in accordance with Jewish law.

Shema: Prayer consisting of verses from Deuteronomy 6:4–9, 11:13–21, and Numbers 15:37–41.

sheva brachot: Seven blessings recited at a Jewish wedding.

shin: ש, A letter of the Hebrew alphabet.

shiva: Seven days of mourning following a person's burial.

shloshim: Literally, "thirty"; thirty-day mourning period following a person's burial.

shofar: Ram's horn.

shul (Yiddish): Synagogue.

Shulchan Aruch: Literally, "a set table"; the code of laws and practices published in 1567 by Joseph Caro of the Galilee (1488–1575), with additions by Moses Isserles of Cracow (1520–70).

siddur: Prayer book.

Talmud: Literally, "teaching"; usually refers to the Babylonian Talmud, completed about 500 CE, a collection of the discussions and decisions of the Rabbis from about 300 to 500 CE. These discussions were an elaboration and clarification of the laws of the *Mishnah*.

tefillah: Prayer.

teshuva: Repentance.

Torah: Handwritten scroll of the Five Books of Moses.

tzitzit: Fringes.

tzom: Fast or fasting.

tzom shtikah: A fast of silence; medieval kabbalistic practice in which one refrains from speaking.

yahrtzeit (Yiddish): Anniversary of a person's death on the Jewish calendar.

yichud: Literally, "privacy" or "union"; term for the private time between the bride and groom that constitutes the final stage of the marriage ceremony.

Yom Kippur: Day of Atonement.

author's note

The names and identifying details of a few of the people who appear in these pages have been changed.